GAYMER'S
COUNTY
GUIDES

OXFORDSHIRE

First published by
Gaymer's Guides Limited,
24 Notting Hill Gate, London W11 3BR
Tel: 01-229 9944 Fax: 01-727 5442

Copyright © Gaymer's Guides Ltd. 1989
Gaymer's County Guides to Oxfordshire
ISBN 1-872173-00-4

Editor: Stephen Gaymer
Assistant Editor: Alison Ritchie
Designer: Angel Bacon

Cover photographs, clockwise:
St. John's Quad, Magdalen College, Oxford;
Garsington Manor; Henley Bridge; Minster Lovell Hall.
Back cover: Oriel College, Oxford.
© AA Photolibrary

Printed by Whitstable Litho Printers Ltd., Whitstable, Kent.
Typeset in Palatino on a Linotronic 300 by Alphabet Set,
Chelsea Wharf, London SW10 0QJ

The publishers would like to thank the
following for their assistance in the compilation of this guide:
Patrick Brown, Sarah Chamberlain, Edward Crawshaw, David Doyle,
Duncan Fraser, Sebastian Grimes, Andrew Lucas, Iain Norton of Norton Associates, John Stimpson.

CONTENTS

KEY TO ABBREVIATIONS

AA.	Automobile Association	Dogs.	Dogs allowed	RAC.	Royal Automobile Club
Ac.	Access	ER.	Egon Ronay	V.	Visa
Am.	American Express	F.	Functions	Veg.	Vegetarian food
B.	Banquets	M.	Michelin Guide		available
CF.	Conference facilities	N/S.	No smoking areas	W.	Weddings
D.	Diners Club	P.	Parties	W/chair.	Wheelchair access

CHARLBURY, OXFORDSHIRE (PAGE 31)

GAYMER'S COUNTY GUIDES are the first fully-illustrated comprehensive guide books that contain a gazetteer of every town, village and hamlet within a given area; they also list every hotel, guest house, restaurant and pub within that area, plus places of interest and churches. Other amenities are also included, such as art galleries, leisure and garden centres, cinemas and theatres, and so on. In short, Gaymer's County Guides list everything that may be of interest to visitors.

There are many publications which list some of these facilities, but none that list them all; they also tend to be selective. Gaymer's County Guides list everything, without qualification. However, by giving more details of certain establishments, it is left to the readers' discretion to decide whether a particular place suits their requirements.

At the back of the book are detailed indexes; the illustrations, the places of interest and towns are indexed alphabetically. Other amenities are cross-referenced, so that should a specific amenity be sought, for example a swimming pool, it can be located. There is a map and an index which shows towns by map reference.

In this edition there is a featured pub and restaurant (see contents). In future editions more establishments will be recommended as they are recommended to us.

The majority of establishments whose full details appear have paid a fee, and will have copies of this guide for sale. Although every effort has been made there will inevitably be places that have been overlooked. We invite readers to send in details of omissions or inaccuracies.

Our aim is to produce a fully comprehensive and accurate representation of every relevant amenity in the area, that will serve as an invaluable aid to tourists and inhabitants alike.

THE THAMES AT OXFORD

AN OXFORD SWAN

ROUSHAM HOUSE, STEEPLE ASTON (PAGE 101)

THE UNIVERSITY of Oxford is known throughout the world as part of man's cultural heritage. Established in 1214, by the end of that century four colleges had been founded, others following until the 19th century, when five women's colleges were founded, creating most of the 653 buildings of architectural interest within one square mile.

The City of Oxford, with its honey-coloured stone, noble lawns and famous 'dreaming spires', stands on the rivers Thames and Cherwell, which help shape the city's life, with those perennial undergraduate pastimes of punting, boating, fishing and bathing. Oxford has been moulded by the University's presence, and in turn exerts its influence on the county which takes its name.

Oxford, city and county, has long been associated with the motor car, being the home of Morris (the Oxford and Cowley are world renowned), and Abingdon, to the south, is birthplace to that best-loved car, the M.G..

Sandwiched between the Cotswolds in the west and the Chilterns in the east, the river Thames winding grandly through its midst, Oxfordshire is a county with a rich array of England's natural beauty in hill, valley and broad plain. It lies close to the centre of the English plain, equidistant to London, Southampton and Bristol, with their great water inlets, and Birmingham to the north.

It is a county of great historical interest, with notable prehistoric, Roman, Saxon and Norman remains. In medieval times the royal hunting forest of Wychwood, in the north-west of the county, was as important as the New Forest, and gave its name to such picturesque villages as Shipton-under-Wychwood and Milton-under-Wychwood. In the middle ages, Cotswold wool was one of England's chief sources of revenue, and the rich wool merchants built a number of impressive churches and stone manor houses. During the Civil War numerous battles and skirmishes were fought in and around Oxfordshire, most notably the Battles of Islip, Cropredy Bridge and Radcot Bridge. Many large houses were Royalist strongholds, Broughton Castle and Faringdon House to name just two, while the manor house at Marston, just outside Oxford, became the national headquarters of the Parliamentary army. Situated at Woodstock is Vanbrugh's magnificent Blenheim Palace, which, among other distinctions, was the birthplace of that most famous Englishman, Sir Winston Churchill.

To the east of the county is an area of wide skies, vast cornfields and stretches of wilderness. Ot Moor, a bleak uninhabited expanse covering six square miles, is ringed by attractive villages. Along the banks of the rivers Thame and Cherwell more pretty villages abound.

In 1974, the new county of Oxfordshire was created, incorporating the old county plus much of North Berkshire. This brought the 'commuter belt' into the county, including the Thameside town of Wallingford, the market town of Wantage, birthplace of Alfred the Great, and such enchanting villages as Blewbury and Goring-on-Thames.

KINGSTON LISLE PARK (PAGE 64)

THE UPPER REACHES, ABINGDON

ABINGDON

Abingdon is the attractive former county town of Berkshire on the River Thames. There are many interesting buildings, including the remains of a once powerful Benedictine abbey, and an imposing Napoleonic prison, now imaginatively converted into a leisure centre. The 17th Century County Hall, built by a pupil of Sir Christopher Wren in 1678, stands on graceful columns in the market place, where there is now a museum in the former Assize court on the first floor. Abingdon prospered in the late Middle Ages with cloth manufacturing and in later centuries, breweries, flour mills and agricultural machine factories flourished. Down by the river a reconstructed Elizabethan theatre stages plays and operas during the summer. There are regular boat trips to Oxford, and craft for hire.

Population: 22,451. Market day: Monday. Early closing: Thursday. Map Ref: C 10.

PLACES OF INTEREST

Abbey Buildings

Benedictine Abbey founded in 690. Twice sacked by the Danes, it was finally completed in about 1170. By the 15th century it was second only in importance to Glastonbury. *Months Open: All Year. Days Open: Daily except Mondays in Oct-March. Hours Open: 2-6. Bank Holidays: Closed.*

Abingdon Museum

The County Hall, Market Place.
Tel: (0235) 23703

Situated on the first floor of the County Hall in the former Assize Court, this museum is dedicated to Abingdon and the history of the surrounding area.
Hours Open: 2-5 pm. Bank Holidays: Closed.

CHURCHES

Christ Church Anglican

Northcote Road. Tel: (0235) 22549

St Edmund (RC)

Radley Road.

St Helen

East St Helen's St.

Built in the 13th century, and remodelled in the 15th and 16th, resulting in a church with five aisles and unusual in being wider than it is long, a rare claim, as only one other church in England has such a characteristic. In the Lady chapel there is a remarkable 14th century roof, and a Jesse tree. The Victorian white marble font was displayed at the Great Exhibition of 1851.

St Mary (RC)

Oxford Road.

St Michael

Park Road.

St Nicholas

Market Place.

Originally built for travellers to the Abbey in the 12th century. The River Stert runs under the nave, and is the Abbey boundary.

HOTELS

The Abingdon Lodge Hotel

Marcham Road. OX14 1TZ Tel: (0235) 553456
A new Hotel with modern facilities.
*BEDROOMS: 32 Double, (32 en suite, 32 TV, 32 phone, 32 tea/
coffee) B&B £ 40.00 - £ 62.00. 31 Twin, (31 en suite, 31 TV, 31
phone, 31 tea/coffee) B&B £ 40.00 - £ 62.00. 2 Suites. RESTAU-
RANT: International Cuisine. Lunch: £ 8.95. Tea: £ 0.65.
Dinner: £ 12.00. House Wine: £ 5.45. À La Carte: £ 10.00.
HOTEL INFORMATION: CF. W. B. F. 85 space Car Park.
Credit Cards: AC. AM. D. V. Recommendations: AA***.*
Weekend Breaks: 2 nights: £ 56.00. 3 nights: £ 84.00.

The Blue Boar Hotel
Bath Street. OX14 3QH Tel: (0235) 23719

The Crown and Thistle
Bridge Street. OX14 3HR Tel: (0235) 22556
An old coaching inn, a listed building, with a cobbled
courtyard. Centrally situated.

The Grapes
28 High Street. OX14 5AX Tel: (0235) 20114

The Nags Head
The Bridge. Tel: (0235) 22965

The Upper Reaches Hotel
Thames Street. OX14 3JA Tel: (0235) 22311
Situated virtually on an island overlooking the Thames,
making it the ideal choice for a quiet relaxing break in
Oxfordshire.
*BEDROOMS: 6 Single,(6 en suite,6 TV, 6 phone,6 tea/coffee)
B&B £ 60.00 11 Double, (11 en suite, 11 TV, 11 phone, 11 tea/
coffee) B&B £ 65.00 - £ 75.00. 3 Twin, (3 en suite, 3 TV, 3 phone,
3 tea/coffee) B&B £ 65.00 - £ 75.00. 4 Family, (4 en suite, 4 TV,
4 phone, 4 tea/coffee) £ 71.00 - £ 83.00. 2 Suites. RESTAU-
RANT: English Cuisine. Lunch: £ 10.75. Tea: £ 2.95. Dinner:
£ 14.95. House Wine: £ 6.25. HOTEL INFORMATION: CF.
W. B. F. 70 space Car Park. Dogs. Credit Cards: AC. AM. D. V.
Recommendations: AA ***. ER. M. RAC ***.*
Weekend Breaks: 2 nights: £ 80.00. 3 nights: £ 120.00.
Allowance towards dinner: £ 11.95.

The Warwick Arms Hotel
Ock Street. OX14 5DQ Tel: (0235) 22974

GUEST HOUSES

Ambleside Lodge
33 Oxford Road. Tel: (0235) 23663

Knowles Guest House
53 Stert Street. Tel: (0235) 28658
A Recently re-furbished period hotel. One hour's drive
from London.
*Months Open: All year. Number of Bedrooms: 18. (15 with
bathroom). B&B per person: £18-28. TV. Pets. Evening meals.
Car park. Garden.*

Oxford Guest House
37 Oxford Road. Tel: (0235) 20151

RESTAURANTS
The Chinese Kitchen (Takeaway)

3 The Square. Tel: (0235) 25941
Il Camino
13 Bath Street. Tel: (0235) 32211
The Kismet Restaurant
20 High Street. Tel: (0235) 25540
*Bangladesh (Indian) Cuisine. Specialities: Mutton or Chicken
Tikka Massala/Tandoori Chicken, King Prawn Massala. Hours
Open: Lunch: 12-2.30. Dinner: 6 - midnight. Last Orders: 12
am. Closed Christmas Day. Open Sundays. Lunch: £ 11.50.
Dinner: £ 11.50. House Wine: £ 5.00. Seating Capacity: 51. Veg.*

Pete's Tropicana
1 Bury Street. Tel: (0235) 34170
The Prince of India Restaurant
10 Ock Street. Tel: (0235) 32856

PUBLIC HOUSES

The Air Balloon
Ock Street. Tel: (0235) 23453
The Barley Mow
Lombard Street. Tel: (0235) 28054
The Beehive
46 Stert Street. Tel: (0235) 20732
The Black Swan
Bath Street. Tel: (0235) 20276
The Blue Boar
Bath Street. Tel: (0235) 23719
Boundary House
Oxford Road. Tel: (0235) 20286
The Broadface
32 Bridge Street. Tel: (0235) 24516
The College Oak Public House
Peachcroft Road. Tel: (0235) 554937
The Cross Keys
Ock Street. Tel: (0235) 21738
The Crown
83 Ock Street. Tel: (0235) 21655
The Fitzharris Arms
Thornhill Walk, Wootton Road. Tel: (0235) 23281
The George & Dragon
Stert Street. Tel: (0235) 20801
A friendly town house. Car park at rear entrance through
archway immediately adjacent to pub.
*Brewery: Morland. Licensee: Mr Peter Fassam. Opening Hours:
Varied opening times. Food Available: 12-2pm.*

The Horse & Jockey
47 Bath Street. Tel: (0235) 52719
*Brewery: Morrells Best Bitter. Opening Hours: 11 am- 11pm.
Food Available: 12 - 2pm   6 - 9pm.*

The Ox Inn
15 Oxford Road. Tel: (0235) 20962
The Prince of Wales
23 Spring Road. Tel: (0235) 29753
The Punchbowl
6 Market Place. Tel: (0235) 20230

THE OLD GAOL LEISURE CENTRE

The Red Lion
63 The Vineyard. Tel: (0235) 21128
The Saxton Arms
Saxton Road. Tel: (0235) 20457
The Spread Eagle
Northcourt Road. Tel: (0235) 21594
The White Horse
Ock Street. Tel: (0235) 24490

TEA ROOMS
Frageo's
2 East St Helen's Street. Tel: (0235) 23260
Miss Marples Tea Shoppe
29 Broad Street. Tel: (0235) 23135
Poppies Tearooms
37 Stert Street. Tel: (0235) 26660
Walters Cafe
152 Ock Street. Tel: (0235) 20134

OTHER AMENITIES
BOAT HIRE
Abingdon Boat Centre
Nags Head Island. OX14 3HX Tel: (0235) 21125
Adventure Hire
The Old Bakery, 62B Bath Street. Tel: (0235) 23191
Red Line Cruisers
Ferry Boat House, Wilsham Road. OX14 5HP
Tel: (0235) 21562
CAR HIRE
Fisher Wedding Cars
3, Francis Little Drive. Tel: (0235) 33088
CAR HIRE/SELF DRIVE

Gowrings of Abingdon
111, Ock Street. Tel: (0235) 26793
Garage
Months Open: 12 months. Days Open: All week. Hours Open:
7 am - 9 pm Mon -Sat 9 am - 5pm Sun. Open Bank Holidays.
Petrol/Diesel sales. New and used cars. Motorcraft centre. MOT
centre. Workshop Proprietor: Geoffrey Allison.
Ridgefield Self Drive Hire
6, Ginge Close. Tel: (0235) 30420
CINEMA
Regal Cinema
The Square. Tel: (0235) 20322
STORE
Woolworths plc
21, Bury Street. Tel: (0235) 20928
GARDEN CENTRE
Sandfords
Fairacres, Marcham Road. Tel: (0235) 21004
HEALTH CLUB
Lifers Health Suite
The Old Jail Leisure Centre, Bridge Street.
Tel: (0235) 34409
HOLIDAY ACCOMODATION
Twickenham House
East St Helen's Street. Tel: (0235) 21087
HOSPITAL
Abingdon Hospital
Marcham Road. Tel: (0235) 22717
LEISURE CENTRES
Old Gaol Leisure Centre
Bridge Street. Tel: (0235) 22806
Oracle Snooker Club

9

West St Helen's Street. Tel: (0235) 30746
Radley College Sports Centre
Abingdon. Tel: (0235) 34116
SNOOKER CENTRE
Oracle Snooker Club
West St Helen's Street. Tel: (0235) 30746
SPORTS CLUBS
Abingdon Bowling Club
Albert Park, Park Road. Tel: (0235) 23402
Abingdon Cricket Club
Hales Meadow. Tel: (0235) 24405
Abingdon Squash Club
Northcourt Road. Tel: (0235) 30374
Abingdon Town F C
Culham Road. Tel: (0235) 21684
Abingdon United F C & Social Club
Northcourt Road. Tel: (0235) 22022
Lansdown Club
11d, Milton Park. Tel: (0235) 831962
YOUTH HOSTEL
Rush Common Hostel
Dorchester Crescent. Tel: (0235) 21703

ϾϪ ϾϪ ϾϪ ϾϪ ϾϪ ϾϪ ϾϪ

ADDERBURY

Owing its original prosperity to the wool trade, Adderbury is a large village that is cut in two by the Sor Brook. There are a number of large and grand houses, including the remains of Adderbury House, once owned by the infamous Restoration poet, John Wilmot, Earl of Rochester. The house was altered in the 18th century and a large part of Adderbury was pulled down to make way for a park. There is a medieval tithe barn. West Adderbury, down by the brook, is quiet and has winding lanes and paths.
Population: 2,381. Map Ref: F 3.

CHURCHES
Friends Meeting House
Methodist Chapel
St Mary
Tel: (0295) 810309
A 12th century church rebuilt in 1790. Described at the time as 'More like a gaol than a Christian Temple'.

PUBLIC HOUSES
The Bell Inn
Tel: (0295) 810338
The Coach & Horses
The Green. Tel: (0295) 810422
The Dog and Partridge
Tel: (0295) 810296

The Plough Inn
Tel: (0295) 810327
The Red Lion Hotel
Tel: (0295) 810269
The White Hart
Tanners Lane. Tel: (0295) 810406
Free House. Recommendations: Good Pub Guide.

OTHER AMENITIES
CAR HIRE/SELF DRIVE
Nell Bridge Filling Station
Aynho Road. Tel: (0295) 812121
MUSEUM
Waterways Art Gallery
Nell Bridge House Farm. Tel: (0295) 811840
SPORTS CLUB
Adderbury Sports Club
Round Close Road. Tel: (0295) 810077

ϾϪ ϾϪ ϾϪ ϾϪ ϾϪ ϾϪ ϾϪ

ALVESCOT
A small village consisting of old stone houses and farm buildings. The church stands on a hill and there is a memorial to an 18th century rector.
Population: 328. Map Ref: B 8.

CHURCH
St Peter

PUBLIC HOUSES
The Plough
Tel: (0993) 842281
The Red Lion
Tel: (0993) 841745

ϾϪ ϾϪ ϾϪ ϾϪ ϾϪ ϾϪ ϾϪ

AMBROSDEN
A Roman camp was based here, and the old village centre is surrounded by large MOD buildings.
Population: 1,244. Map Ref: H 6.

CHURCH
St Mary

PUBLIC HOUSE
The Turner Arms
Tel: (0869) 252468

ϾϪ ϾϪ ϾϪ ϾϪ ϾϪ ϾϪ ϾϪ

APPLEFORD
A village with two sets of developments, some old

houses, some new houses, a pub, a church, a small railway station and small greens.

Population: 395. Map Ref: F 11.

CHURCH
St Peter & St Paul
Simple Late Norman doorway and a 13th century chancel. In the graveyard is buried one John Faulkener, by repute the worlds oldest jockey, who won his last race aged 74.

PUBLIC HOUSE
The Carpenters Arms
Main Road. Tel: (0235) 848328

🐾 🐾 🐾 🐾 🐾 🐾 🐾

APPLETON
A mixed village of brick and stone situated below Cumnor Hill. Appleton Manor is 12th century with a Norman doorway worthy of any church, and Tudor additions. The Post Office dates from 1690. In the 19th century one of the leading businesses was bell-making.

Population: 844. Map Ref: E9.

CHURCH
St Lawrence
The church is mostly Norman, with a 15th century tower and some later additions.

PUBLIC HOUSES
The Plough Inn
Tel: (0865) 862441
The Thatched Tavern
Tel: (0865) 862065
The Three Horseshoes
Tel: (0865) 862130

🐾 🐾 🐾 🐾 🐾 🐾 🐾

ARDINGTON
The first village east of Wantage, which, along with its twin model village Lockinge, was planned, restored and rebuilt by Lord Wantage who was one of the first Victoria Cross winners in the Crimean War. A school, rectory and Inn are grouped around the old church.

Population: 284. Map Ref: D11.

PLACES OF INTEREST
Ardington House
Tel: (02365) 833244
Ardington House is a Georgian house with gardens, once owned by Lord Wantage, built in red and grey Berkshire

brick and is open to the public during the summer . The main feature is two staircases which join into one.

Months Open: May-September. Days Open: Mondays. Hours Open: 2.30-4.30pm.

CHURCH
Holy Trinity
A12th century church, which was over-restored in 1847; there are carved heads on the tower and a Norman doorway. There is a statue of a kneeling woman by Baily, who designed Nelson's Column.

PUBLIC HOUSE
The Boars Head
Tel: (0235) 833254

OTHER AMENITIES
FISH FARM
Lockinge Fishery
Tel: (0235) 833200

🐾 🐾 🐾 🐾 🐾 🐾 🐾

ARNCOTT
Population: 987. Map Ref: H6.

PUBLIC HOUSES
The Plough
Ploughly Road. Tel: (0869) 252379
The Tally Ho
Tel: (0869) 247170

🐾 🐾 🐾 🐾 🐾 🐾 🐾

ASCOTT-UNDER-WYCHWOOD
In the Evenlode Valley, stands this little grey stone village with a Norman church. The word Wychwood refers to the royal forest which stretched some 12 miles between Bladon and Burford.

Population: 476. Map Ref: B5.

CHURCH
Holy Trinity
A small rustic church built around 1200.

🐾 🐾 🐾 🐾 🐾 🐾 🐾

ASHBURY
A village on the Downs with interesting chalk and thatched buildings, a manor house, a country inn and a large church overlooking the Vale of Ashbury. A good centre for exploring the Ridgeway.

Population: 523. Map Ref: A12.

PLACES OF INTEREST

ASHDOWN HOUSE, ASHBURY

Ashdown House
Tel: (0494) 28051

An unusual 17th century house built by Lord Craven for Elizabeth of Bohemia, but she died before she could live there. It has a roof crowned by a cupola and a golden ball with spectacular views over the Downs. In the grounds there are some sarsen stones called 'Merlin's Sheep' similar to ones at Avebury and Stonehenge.

Months Open: Woodlands: All year. House & garden: April - October. Days Open: Woodlands: Daily except Friday. House & Garden: Wednesday and Saturdays. Hours Open: Woodlands: Dawn-Dusk. House & Garden: 2-6pm. Closed Easter Saturday and Bank Holiday Mondays.

Waylands Smithy
A megalithic long barrow, a prehistoric burial place surrounded by sarsen stones, a long earthen mound containing a chamber made of large blocks of stone. Legend has it that any horse left at the entrance will be shod by Wayland, blacksmith to the Saxon gods, if a coin is left on the lintel.
Months Open: All Year. Days Open: Every Day. Hours Open: Dawn-Dusk. Bank Holidays: Open.

CHURCH
St Mary
Norman church with additions throughout the centuries.

HOTEL
The Rose and Crown Hotel
SN6 8NA Tel: (079 371) 222

A pleasant country Inn, offering friendly service, warm and comfortable.

🐾 🐾 🐾 🐾 🐾 🐾 🐾

ASTHALL
On the banks of the gentle River Windrush, this delightful village boasts a Jacobean manor house built in 1620 with mullioned windows, which looks across the churchyard and down to the old river bridge. On the top of the hill is a Saxon burial place called Asthall Barrow.
Population: 228. Map Ref: B 7.

CHURCH
St. Nicholas
Contains a 14th century effigy of Lady Joan Cornwall and some medieval stained glass in its chantry chapel.

HOTEL
The Maytime Inn
Tel: (099 382) 2068

RESTAURANT
The Windmill Restaurant
Windrush Valley Park. Tel: (099 382) 2594

🐾 🐾 🐾 🐾 🐾 🐾 🐾

ASTON (BERKS)

Situated on the River Thames, Aston is a hamlet which has a picturesque inn on the site of a ferry. *Map Ref: K13.*

HOTEL

The Flowerpot Hotel

RG9 3DG Tel: (0491) 574721

Victorian pub originally catering for fishing and boating parties. Secluded location near to the River Thames, with an attractive garden and its own landing stage.

🐦 🐦 🐦 🐦 🐦 🐦 🐦

ASTON (OXON)

A small hamlet between Bampton & Standlake. *Map Ref: C 9.*

PUBLIC HOUSES

The Bull Inn

Bull Street. Tel: (0993) 850252

The Red Lion

Tel: (0993) 850491

🐦 🐦 🐦 🐦 🐦 🐦 🐦

ASTON ROWANT

Probably named after one Rowland de Easton, who owned land here in 1242. The grounds of Aston House now contain houses. The presence of Aston Park Stud ensures that horses abound in this little village. *Population: 833. Map Ref: K 10.*

PLACES OF INTEREST

Nature Reserve

The whole of the Chiltern Hills has been designated as an Area of Outstanding Natural Beauty. This nature reserve is on one of the highest ridges of the Chilterns.

🐦 🐦 🐦 🐦 🐦 🐦 🐦

ASTON TIRROLD

Situated below the Downs near Streatley, Aston Tirrold is a charming village with half-timbered houses, thatched cottages and a 14th century church. It stands in the shelter of Blewburton Hill, the ancient hill fort. There has been speculation that Alfred's great victory over the Danes at Ashdown, was in fact fought on the Downs above Aston. There is a Queen Anne manor house near the church, the eastern part dating from 1740 with a Shell Porch; other parts have been added later, but in style.

Population: 370. Map Ref: G 12.

CHURCHES

Presbyterian Chapel

In Spring Lane, posssibly on the site of England's oldest nonconformist chapel.

St Michael

St Michael has a Norman doorway and an even earlier doorway leading into the vestry.

PUBLIC HOUSE

Chequers

Tel: (0235) 850253

🐦 🐦 🐦 🐦 🐦 🐦 🐦

ASTON UPTHORPE

Twinned with Aston Tirrold, the name actually means 'upper village'. The church is a simple nave and chancel building with various Norman features. Nearby Blewburton Hill has an Iron Age fort on top of it and is a good walking area. King Alfred's brother Ethelred reputedly prayed in the church here while Alfred attacked the Danes from Blewburton Hill.

Population: 178. Map Ref: G 12.

CHURCH

All Saints

PUBLIC HOUSE

The Boot

Thorpe Street. Tel: (0235) 850208

🐦 🐦 🐦 🐦 🐦 🐦 🐦

AYNHO

A village made largely of local limestone. Apricot trees line the streets, and the fruit was for years taken as a toll by the Lord of the Manor, who lived at nearby Aynho Park.

Map Ref: G 3.

PLACES OF INTEREST

Aynho Park

Tel: (0869) 810636

Large 17th century house standing in the village centre, a few rooms open to the public.

Months Open: May- September. Days Open: Wednesday & Thursday.

HOTEL

The Cartright Arms Hotel

Tel: (0869) 810218

BALSCOTE

Map Ref: D 1.

CHURCH
St Mary Magdalene

PUBLIC HOUSE
The Butchers Arms
Tel: (0295) 730750

🐾 🐾 🐾 🐾 🐾 🐾 🐾

BAMPTON

Home of Morris Dancing, this riverside parish, formerly known as Bampton-in-the-Bush, provides an ideal base for touring the Cotswolds, the Vale of the White Horse and the Upper Thames Valley. An important market town until the 18th century, it was famous for its horse fair. The prettiest part of the village surrounds the churchyard,where are grouped the stately manor house, old rectory and a deanery once owned by the Dean of Exeter. There is an annual Morris Dancing festival which attracts many visitors and dancers. Bampton has many quaint inns and elegant Georgian houses, which gives it the feel of a small market town, rather than a large village.

Population: 1,948. Early closing: Thursday. Map Ref: B 9.

CHURCHES
Methodist Chapel
St Mary
St Mary's is one of the largest churches in West Oxfordshire. The 170ft spire is a landmark for miles around. It is mainly 13th century, and has many beautiful windows but it was destructively restored inside in the 19th century. Found within the church is a copy of the deed given to the Bishop of Exeter by William the Conqueror, entitling him to the Manor of Bampton and all the land stretching southeast to the river Thames.

HOTEL
The Talbot Hotel
Market Place. Tel: (0993) 850326

RESTAURANTS
The Poachers Restaurant
Market Square. Tel: (0993) 850020
The Romany Inn
Bridge Street . Tel: (0993) 850237

PUBLIC HOUSES
The Eagle
Church View. Tel: (0993) 850279

The Elephant & Castle
Bridge Street. Tel: (0993) 850316
Licensee: Mr H Rainey.
The George & Dragon
Broad Street. Tel: (0993) 850410
The Horse Shoe Inn
Bridge Street. Tel: (0993) 850201
The Jubilee Inn
Tel: (0993) 850330
Brewery: Wadworths. Licensee: Mrs Cynthia Locke. Opening Hours: 11am - 2.30 pm 6 pm - 11 pm. Food Available: 12 - 2 pm 7 - 9.30pm . Garden.

🐾 🐾 🐾 🐾 🐾 🐾 🐾

BANBURY

Founded in Saxon times, Banbury is the second largest town in Oxfordshire, and the undisputed capital of the northern part of the county. Famous for its cattle market (this has now been moved to a site near the railway station) which is the largest in England, handling 600,000 head of livestock a year, also for its dried spice fruit cakes, and of course,the nursery rhyme 'Banbury Cross'. In fact the original Crosses (as contrary to popular belief, there were in fact three crosses) were destroyed in 1602, and the one now standing in the town centre was erected in 1859. The 12th century castle, built by the Bishop of Lincoln, was also destroyed in 1648 to provide materials to repair damage caused by two destructive Civil War sieges. A medieval church used to stand in Banbury, with all the characteristics of Perpendicular architecture, but in the 18th century the decision was made to destroy it completely due to its total state of disrepair. It was then replaced in 1793 by the present Classical Georgian church. The woollen trade in the late Middle Ages brought great prosperity to Banbury, helped further by the opening of the Oxford Canal in 1778, and the building of a railway in the next century. Ideally situated on routes from the Midlands to the south, Banbury is a thriving industrial, marketing and shopping centre. There are some fine houses, and interesting old inns.

Population: 35,796. Market day: Thursday/Saturday. Early closing: Tuesday. Map Ref: F 2.

PLACES OF INTEREST
Banbury Museum
8, Horsefair.
Tel: (0295) 59855
Local history museum. Includes a display on Banbury Castle when it stood, and has a feature on 'Banburyshire' with Banbury as the focal point of the surrounding area.

Months Open: All Year. Days Open: Ring for exact days. Hours Open: Ring for exact times. Bank Holidays: Closed Good Friday, and Christmas/Boxing day.

Sulgrave Manor House
Tel: (029 576) 205

Ancestral home of George Washington; the family's coat of arms is said to have inspired the Stars and Stripes. There is a small museum of Washington memorabilia, and in the 14th century church is the tomb of Laurence Washington, who built the house.

Bank Holidays: Closed Christmas Day & Boxing Day.

CHURCHES

Baptist Chapel
Horsefair.

Cemetary Chapel
Southam Road.

Congregational Chapel
South Bar Street.

Banbury Methodist Church
Marlborough Road. Tel: (0295) 57193

St John (RC)
South Bar Street.

St Joseph's Presbytery
Edmunds Road. Tel: (0295) 4661

St Mary's Centre
Horsefair. Tel: (0295) 53329

HOTELS

The Banbury Cross Inn
Butchers Row. Tel: (0295) 53210

The Banbury Moat House
29 Oxford Road. 0X16 9AH Tel: (0295) 59361

Elegant Georgian building, situated close to town centre. Newly renovated and offers modern amenities. The hotel has a warm and friendly atmosphere.

*BEDROOMS: 10 Single, (10 en suite, 10 TV, 10 phone, 10 tea/coffee) B&B £ 48.00 - £ 55.00. 22 Double, (22 en suite, 22 TV, 22 phone, 22 tea/coffee) B&B £ 50.00 - £ 65.00. 12 Twin, (12 en suite, 12 TV, 12 phone, 12 tea/coffee) B&B £ 50.00 - £ 65.00. 3 Family, (3 en suite, 3 TV, 3 phone, 3 tea/coffee) £ 50.00 - £ 75.00. 1 Four Poster, £ 85.00. RESTAURANT: English/French Cuisine. HOTEL INFORMATION: CF. W. B. F. 40 space Car Park: Credit Cards: AC. AM. D. V. Recommendations: AA ***. ER. M. RAC ***.*

Weekend Breaks: 2 nights: £ 66.00. 3 nights: £ 99.00. Allowance towards dinner: £ 9.50.

The Coach & Horses
Butchers Row. OX16 8JH Tel: (0295) 3043

The Cromwell Lodge
North Bar. OX16 0TB Tel: (0295) 59781

Well equipped bedrooms attractive restaurant, good food.

Easington House Hotel
50 Oxford Road. OX16 9AN Tel: (0295) 270181

The Lismore Hotel
61 Oxford Road. 0X16 9AJ Tel: (0295) 62105

The Marlborough Arms
Gatteridge Street. OX16 8DJ Tel: (0295) 58258

Whately Hall Hotel
Horsefair. OX16 0AN Tel: (0295) 3451

Situated in beautifully manicured gardens, and directly opposite the famous Banbury Cross, Whately Hall is a careful blend of old and new. Dating back to 1632 this historic hotel has many fine old rooms with oak beams and secret staircases.

*BEDROOMS: 17 Single, (17 en suite, 17 phone, 17 tea/coffee) B&B £ 60.00 - £ 70.00. 21 Double, (21 en suite, 21 TV, 21 phone, 21 tea/coffee) B&B £ 80.00 - £ 90.00. 22 Twin, (22 en suite, 22 TV, 22 phone, 22 tea/coffee) B&B £ 80.00 - £ 90.00. 14 Family, (14 en suite, 14 TV, 14 phone, 14 tea/coffee) £ 100.00 - £ 130.00. 2 Suites. RESTAURANT: Traditional Cuisine. Lunch: £ 9.00. Tea: £ 3.50. Dinner: £ 15.00. House Wine: £ 8.00. À La Carte: £ 10.00. Specialities: Traditional local dishes. HOTEL INFORMATION: CF. W. B. F. 70 space Car Park: Dogs. NS. 16th Century. Credit Cards: AC. AM. D. V. Recommendations: AA***. ER.*

Weekend Breaks: 2 nights: £ 74.00. 3 nights: £ 111.00.

The White Lion Hotel
High Street. OX16 8JW Tel: (0295) 4358

GUEST HOUSES

Amberley Guest House
151 Middleton Road. Tel: (0295) 55797

Belmont Guest House
34 Crouch Street. Tel: (0295) 62308

Calthorpe Lodge Guest House
4 Calthorpe Road. Tel: (0295) 52325

Cotswold Guest House
45 Oxford Road. Tel: (0295) 56414

Fairlawns Guest House
60 Oxford Road. Tel: (0295) 62461

Fairview Lodge
1 Fairview Road. OX16 8HU. Tel: (0295) 62181

Fernleigh Guest House
67 Oxford Road. Tel: (0295) 50645

Kelvedon Guest House
11 Broughton Road. Tel: (0295) 3028

Friendly comfortable guest house. A few minutes from Banbury Cross.

Months Open: All year. Number of Bedrooms: 4. (1 with bathroom). B&B per person: £13. TV. Pets. Car Park. Garden.

The Plush Guest House
4 Middleton Road. Tel: (0295) 52329

Prospect House Guest House
70 Oxford Road. Tel: (0295) 68749

Thomas House Guest House
49 Oxford Road. Tel: (0295) 65903

Tredis Guest House

15 Broughton Road. Tel: (0295) 4632
Treetops Guest House
28 Dashwood Road. Tel: (0295) 54444

RESTAURANTS

The Bamboo Garden Chinese Restaurant
48 Bridge Street. Tel: (0295) 4904

The Banbury Cross Tea Rooms
6 Horse Fair. Tel: (0295) 66720

The Banbury Kebab and Steak House
7 Market Place. Tel: (0295) 53166

The Blacklock Arms
Middleton Road. Tel: (0295) 62776

Capers Hamburgers & Pizza Parlour
7 South Bar. Tel: (0295) 61586

The Flying Horse
Parsons Street. Tel: (0295) 51820
Hours Open: Lunch: 12-2.30pm. Tea: 6.00pm. Dinner: 10.30pm. Last Orders: 10.15pm. Closed 3.00pm - 6.00 pm. Open Sundays. Credit Cards: AC. AM. D. V. Seating Capacity: 100. Vegetarian. Parties.

The Granary Restaurant
6 Butchers Road. Tel: (0295) 50628

Lanes Coffee House
10 Church Street. Tel: (0295) 52918

Lin Hong Chinese Restaurant
53 High Street. Tel: (0295) 3664

Little Chef
A423 Oxford Road. Tel: (0295) 56115

McDonalds
27 Bridge Street. Tel: (0295) 4009

The Mogul Tandoori
58 Parsons Street. Tel: (0295) 51920

Muswells
38 Bridge Street. Tel: (0295) 270151
English/American/Mexican Cuisine. Specialities: Cocktail Bar, Theme Nights. Friendly staff. Lunch: £ 4.00. Tea: £ 1.80. Dinner: £ 8.00. House Wine: £ 5.50. Credit Cards: AC. AM. D. V. Seating Capacity: 80. Vegetarian. Wheelchair. Parties.

Nam Fong
13/14 South Bar. Tel: (0295) 51155

The Peking House Restaurant
80-84 Warwick Road. Tel: (0295) 65614
Peking and Cantonese Cuisine. Hours Open: Lunch: 12-2. Dinner: 5-11. Last Orders: 11. Lunch: £ 5.90. House Wine: £ 5.50. Credit Cards: AC. AM. D. V. Seating Capacity: 70. Wheelchair. Banquets. Parties. Weddings.

Poppins Restaurant
21 Castle Centre. Tel: (0295) 51368

Prince of India
39a Parsons Street. Tel: (0295) 58822

Sarah's Restaurant
28a Castle Centre. Tel: (0295) 56199

The Shish Mahal Tandoori
45 Bridge Street. Tel: (0295) 66489
Genuine Indian Cuisine. Specialities: Clay-Oven - Massalas - Biryany and curries. Hours Open: Lunch: 12-2.30pm. Dinner: 6.00pm-12.00am. Last Orders: 11.45 pm. Closed Christmas and Boxing Day. Open Sundays. Tea: £ 0.80. Dinner: £ 10.45. House Wine: £ 6.95. Credit Cards: AC. AM. D. V. Seating Capacity: 70. Vegetarian. Wheelchair. Banquet. Parties. Weddings. Recommendations: M.

Thai Orchid Restaurant
27 Parsons Street. Tel: (0295) 270833

Vichi Restaurant
16 Broad Street. Tel: (0295) 62969

Wimpey
45 High Street. Tel: (0295) 4675

The Wincott Brasserie
46/47 Bridge Street. Tel: (0295) 67464

PUBLIC HOUSES

The Admiral Holland
Woodgreen Avenue. OX16 0AU Tel: (0295) 65043
Licensee: Mr J S Fisher.

The Barley Mow
Warwick Road. Tel: (0295) 730650

The Bell Inn
Middleton Road. Tel: (0295) 53169

The Bowling Green
Overthorpe Road. Tel: (0295) 3465

The Buck & Bell
North Bar. Tel: (0295) 51390

The Cockhorse
Chatsworth Drive. Tel: (0295) 51271

The Constitution Tavern
Broughton Road. Tel: (0295) 3961

The Dog & Gun
North Bar. Tel: (0295) 62050

The Duke of Wellington
101 Warwick Road. Tel: (0295) 3074

Easington Hotel
135 Bloxham Road. Tel: (0295) 55269

The Globe Inn
Calthorpe St. Tel: (0295) 3469

The Horse & Jockey
10 West Bar. Tel: (0295) 62961

The Jolly Weavers
South Bar. Tel: (0295) 4150

The Musketeer
Ruscote Avenue. Tel: (0295) 57123

The Prince of Wales
Centre Street. Tel: (0295) 3973

The Reindeer Inn
47 Parsons Street. Tel: (0295) 4031

The Three Pigeons
Southam Road. Tel: (0295) 3806
Country Inn. Easy access to M40 and Oxford. Secluded.

Brewery: Halls Oxford and West Brewery Co Ltd. Licensee: Mr Ron Allen. Opening Hours: 9am - 11 pm Closed 3 - 6pm. Food Available: 9 am - 2 pm 6 - 11 pm. 3 Bedrooms: B&B per person: £25. Garden. Children's area.

The Unicorn Hotel
Market Place. Tel: (0295) 3396

The Wheatsheaf Inn
George Street. Tel: (0295) 66525

The White Swan
South Bar. Tel: (0295) 62900

The Woolpack
Church Street. Tel: (0295) 62915

TEA ROOMS

The Bus Station Café
Castle Street. Tel: (0295) 4959

Country Fayre
46 High Street. Tel: (0295) 68521

The Geranium Tea Shoppe
13 White Lion Walk. Tel: (0295) 57966

Tina's Snack bar
6 Church Lane. Tel: (0295) 54160

OTHER AMENITIES

ANTIQUES
Sunloch Gallery
10, West Bar. OX16 9RR Tel: (0295) 55746

BUS & COACH SERVICES
Birmingham & Midland Motor Omnibus
Canal Street. Tel: (0295) 53451

J H Armstrong
61, Mold Crescent. Tel: (0295) 50271

Midland Red (South) Ltd
Castle Street. Tel: (0295) 62368

CAR HIRE/SELF DRIVE
Bridge Motors (Banbury) Ltd
8, Middleton Road. Tel: (0295) 3551

Newtown Car and Van Hire
White Motor Co, Southam Road. Tel: (0295) 58126

Target Car & Van Hire
1, Canal Street. Tel: (0295) 272777

CINEMA
Cannon
Horsefair. Tel: (0295) 62071

STORES
Banbury Trading Post
52-54, Bridge Street. Tel: (0295) 270369

Littlewoods
19/23 Bridge Street, Cherwell Centre. Tel: (0295) 62848

Marks and Spencers Plc
Bridge Street. Tel: (0295) 67676

McIlroys William
Church Lane. Tel: (0295) 62848

GARDEN CENTRES

Boxhedge Nurseries
Boxhedge Road. Tel: (0295) 62146

Clows (Banbury) Ltd
Castle Gardens, Compton Road. Tel: (0295) 66300

Lamprey & Son Ltd
Duke Street. Tel: (0295) 51744

HEALTH CLUB
Banbury Body Studio
2, Mill Lane. Tel: (0295) 53598

HOSPITAL
Horton General Hospital
Banbury. Tel: (0295) 4521

LEISURE CENTRES
Showboat Entertainments Ltd
10, Parsons Street. Tel: (0295) 3030

Spiceball Park Sports Centre
Tel: (0295) 57522
Sports Centre
Months Open: All year. Days Open: All week. Hours Open: 9 .00 am - 10.30 pm (9.30 pm Saturdays). Sundays 10.00 am - 5.30 pm. Large range of activities. Rates: On application. Proprietor: Mrs K White

RAILWAY STATION
Banbury - Parcels and Red Star
Tel: (0295) 62259

SAILING CLUB
Banbury Cross Sailing Club
Tel: (0295) 3928

Tyeki Sun Studio
14b, Bridge Street. Tel: (0295) 270146

SNOOKER CENTRE
Spectrum Snooker Club
10-13 Broad Street, Christchurch Court.
Tel: (0295) 682298

SPORTS CLUBS
Banbury Borough Bowling Club
Peoples Park, Warwick Road. Tel: (0295) 4336

Banbury Chestnuts Bowling Club
The Shades. Tel: (0295) 4123

Banbury Cricket Club
Grange Road. Tel: (0295) 4368

Banbury Rugby Union Football Club
Oxford Road. Tel: (0295) 3862

Banbury Twenty Cricket Club
Daventry Road. Tel: (0295) 3757

Banbury United Supporters Club
Tuston House, Station Approach. Tel: (0295) 50525

British Rail Sports Club
Middleton Road. Tel: (0295) 3395

SWIMMING POOL
Park Road Swimming Pool
Park Road. Tel: (0295) 62742

TOURIST OFFICE
Banbury Tourist Information Centre

Banbury Museum, 8 Horsefair. Tel: (0295) 59855
WINE BAR
Anaconda
23 Cornhill, Market Place. Tel: (0295) 3711

2▲ 2▲ 2▲ 2▲ 2▲ 2▲ 2▲

BARFORD ST MICHAEL

An ironstone village along the Swere valley, with lanes running down a hill to the river and golden brown cottages and houses. There is a thatched inn which has a date of 1679.
Population: 552. Map Ref: E 3.

CHURCHES
Methodist Chapel
St Michaels
Stands on a hill with a Norman tower and two doorways.

PUBLIC HOUSE
The George Inn
Tel: (0869) 38226

2▲ 2▲ 2▲ 2▲ 2▲ 2▲ 2▲

BARNARD GATE

Map Ref: D 7.

GUEST HOUSE
M F & A Gibbons
Ambury Close Farm Tel: (0865) 881356

PUBLIC HOUSE
The Britannia
Tel: (0993) 881231

2▲ 2▲ 2▲ 2▲ 2▲ 2▲ 2▲

BECKLEY

Standing on a 400 ft hill, Beckley has good views over the moor and has stone thatched cottages. Beckley Park has the remains of three moats, and belonged in the 9th century to King Alfred.
Population: 594. Map Ref: G 7.

CHURCH
St. Mary
A Norman church rebuilt in 14th-15th century. The glass is medieval and there are some interesting paintings on the walls.

PUBLIC HOUSE
The Abingdon Arms
Tel: (086735) 311

BENSON

On a plain by the Thames, Benson was once an important halt between Henley and Oxford. A massive red brick 18th century barn with seven entrances with a roof covering an acre is still used for agricultural purposes. RAF Benson nearby houses the Queen's Flight. There is an unusual bicycle museum.
Population: 3,963. Map Ref: H 11.

PLACES OF INTEREST
Benson Cycle Museum
61, Brook Street.
Tel: (0491) 38414
A museum exhibiting a collection of old bicycles from the period 1810 to 1930.
Months Open: By appointment.

CHURCH
St Helen

HOTEL
The Crown
High Street. Tel: (0491) 38247

RESTAURANT
Rivers Night Club & Restaurant
1 St Helen's Avenue. Tel: (0491) 38331

PUBLIC HOUSES
London Road Inn
Beggarbush Lane. Tel: (0491) 35250
The Sun
Watlington Road. Tel: (0491) 35087

OTHER AMENITIES
BOAT HIRE
Benson Cruisers
OX9 8JS Tel: (0491) 38304
CARAVAN PARK
Benson Cruisers
OX9 8JS Tel: (0491) 38304

2▲ 2▲ 2▲ 2▲ 2▲ 2▲ 2▲

BERINSFIELD

A New Town built in 1960 on the site of a war-time airfield.
Map Ref: G 10.

CHURCH
St Mary & St Berrin
Built in 1962 , designed by the Vicar of Dorchester.

OTHER AMENITIES

LEISURE CENTRE
Abbey Sports Centre
Green Furlong. OX9 8LZ Tel: (0865) 341035

🐾 🐾 🐾 🐾 🐾 🐾 🐾

BERRICK SALOME

This quaintly-named village has a little church which was restored in 1890 in a cottagey style.
Population: 152. Map Ref: H 11.

CHURCH
St Helen

🐾 🐾 🐾 🐾 🐾 🐾 🐾

BICESTER

Always a very important crossroads town, Bicester grew from its origins in the 6th century to be a trading centre for the surrounding area, and by the 1700's held no less than seven annual fairs. The industries of the time included wool-combing, chair-making, leatherwork, bell-casting and straw-plaiting. There has been a lot of modern development in Bicester, but the old market place, the focal point of the town, contains most of the town's surviving architectural features, namely half-timbered 16th and 17th century buildings. Some of the roadsides have wide grass verges for the convenience of horseriders.
Population: 14,436. Market day: Monday/Friday Cattle - Friday. Early closing: Thursday. Map Ref: H 5.

CHURCHES
Congregational Chapel
Chapel Street.
Immaculate Conception (RC)
Methodist Chapel
Sheep Street.
St Eadberg
St Eadburg's church, although dating from the 12th century, incorporates Saxon elements and was dedicated to a holy nun called St Eadburga, a cult figure in Saxon times.

HOTELS

The Kings Arms Hotel
Market Square. OX6 7AH Tel: (0869) 249040
The Littlebury Hotel
Kings End . OX6 7DR Tel: (0869) 252595

RESTAURANTS

Courtyard Wine Bar
Market Square. Tel: (0869) 245970

Deans Restaurant
3 Deans Court. Tel: (0869) 253370
Little Chef
A41. Tel: (0869) 245930
The Littlebury Hotel
Kings End. Tel: (0869) 252595
The Sahana Tandoori Restaurant
15 Market Square. Tel: (0869) 245170
Indian Cuisine. Specialities: Balti. Hours Open: Lunch: 12pm Dinner: 6pm. Last Orders: 11.45pm. Credit Cards: AC. AM. D. V. Seating Capacity: 40. Vegetarian. Wheelchair facilities .Banquets. Parties. Weddings.
Taj Mahal Tandoori Restaurant
8 The Causeway. Tel: (0869) 246640
Toppers
25 The Causeway. Tel: (0869) 253921
Wimpey
13 Market Square. Tel: (0869) 246885
Yin Hong Chinese Restaurant
63 Sheep Street. Tel: (0869) 245818

PUBLIC HOUSES

The Angel Inn
102 Sheep Street. Tel: (0869) 252395
The Bell Inn
Sheep Street. Tel: (0869) 252220
The Plough Inn
North Street. Tel: (0869) 249083
The Red Lion
Market Square. Tel: (0869) 253180
The Shakespeare
Shakespeare Drive. Tel: (0869) 240377
The Six Bells
Church Street. Tel: (0869) 253578
The Star Inn
Bucknell Road. Tel: (0869) 253289
The Sun Inn
Church Street. Tel: (0869) 253162
The White Hart Inn
Sheep Street. Tel: (0869) 252789
The White Horse
Churchill Road, Glory Farm Estate. Tel: (0869) 253135

OTHER AMENITIES

HOSPITAL
Bicester Hospital
Tel: (0869) 244881
LEISURE CENTRE
Bicester and Ploughley Sports Centre
Queens Avenue. OX6 8NR Tel: (0869) 253914
Sport and Leisure
Months Open: All Year. Days Open: Seven days a week. Hours Open: 9.00 am - 10.30 pm. Open all Bank Holidays apart from Boxing day. Badminton. Keep fit. Netball. Volleyball. Basket-

ball. Gymnastics. Cricket. Nets. Tennis. Judo. Tang-so-doo. Table tennis. Four squash courts. Four sunbeds. Sauna. Spa bath. 25 x 12.5m heated swimming pool. Floodlit five-a-side. Synthetic grass. Matchpoint bar. Refreshment area. Proprietor: Mr K B Walton.

RAILWAY STATION
Bicester Parcels and Red Star
Tel: (0869) 252018

SNOOKER CENTRE
Bicester Snooker Club
The Old Chapel, Chapel Street. Tel: (0869) 246066

ᘒ ᘒ ᘒ ᘒ ᘒ ᘒ ᘒ

BINFIELD HEATH
Binfield Heath is a small hamlet at the southernmost part of Oxfordshire.
Map Ref: J 14.

PUBLIC HOUSE
The Bottle & Glass
Tel: (0491) 575755
Recommendations: Good Pub Guide.

ᘒ ᘒ ᘒ ᘒ ᘒ ᘒ ᘒ

BIX
Derived from the word meaning hedge, this little village between Henley and Oxford stands on one of the first dual-carriageways built in the country; the toll house bears witness to the importance of the road to London. Set among dense woodland and rolling hills, there are fine views over the Stonor Valley.
Population: 668. Map Ref: J 13.

PUBLIC HOUSE
The Fox Inn
Tel: (0491) 574134

ᘒ ᘒ ᘒ ᘒ ᘒ ᘒ ᘒ

BLACK BOURTON
There is some confusion as to the exact origin of the odd name of this ancient settlement, but it probably had something to do with the monks of Osney who possessed the land from 1180 onwards.
Map Ref: B 8.

CHURCH
St Mary Virgin
BLACKTHORN
Population: 679. Map Ref: I 6.

PUBLIC HOUSES
The Rose & Crown
Tel: (0869) 252534
The Royal Oak Inn
Station Road. Tel: (0869) 252337

ᘒ ᘒ ᘒ ᘒ ᘒ ᘒ ᘒ

BLADON
A neat village of dry-stone walls, limestone and tile buildings on the southern perimeter of Blenheim Park. In the village churchyard is the plain white gravestone of Sir Winston Churchill, surrounded by the graves of other members of the Marlborough family.
Map Ref: E 7.

CHURCHES
Methodist Chapel
St Martin
The original parish church of Woodstock. It become so decayed in 1804 that the Duke of Marlborough ordered a new church. It was again virtually rebuilt in 1891.

PUBLIC HOUSE
The White House Inn
Tel: (0993) 811582
The nearest coach and car park for viewing Sir Winston Churchill's grave. 3 minutes walk to Blenheim Palace.
Brewery: Allied - Ind Coope. Licensee: Mr Leslie Evans. Opening Hours: 10 am - 3 pm 6 - 11 pm. Food Available: Snacks all day. Full menu. Specialities: Gammon steaks cut to order. Large garden. Children's area.

ᘒ ᘒ ᘒ ᘒ ᘒ ᘒ ᘒ

BLETCHINGDON
A small village on a high ridge with good views of Otmoor and the Oxford Canal. There is a green surrounded by cottages , and some 17th century houses. Bletchingdon Park, now a School of English Studies, is an 18th century Palladian mansion built on the site of a Royalist stronghold in the Civil War.
Population: 800. Map Ref: F 6.

CHURCH
St Giles
A small church heavily restored in 1878 from plans made by Charles Buckeridge.

ᘒ ᘒ ᘒ ᘒ ᘒ ᘒ ᘒ

BAY TREE HOTEL

If it was not a hotel the Bay Tree could almost be another tourist attraction in the heart of Burford. The building was completed in the 16th century and boasts a facade of rich Cotswold Stone - as photogenic, in its own way, as the famous high street in Burford with all its antique shops and other boutiques.

Inside this historic building you will find a host of antiques dotted around the public rooms, which set the scene for a memorable visit to one of the Cotswold's most charming and traditional hotels. Here, informality, friendliness and professional service are all part of the hospitality you can expect.

There are twenty two bedrooms, of which three have four-poster beds and another two have their own private sitting rooms. You will find all the usual up to date facilities in the rooms that you would expect, and still the tariff offers remarkably good value for money.

Eating at the Bay Tree can be an exceptional experience. Traditional English cooking is complemented by a wide ranging and informative wine list. The flagstone-floored dining room is open every day for breakfast, lunch and dinner and is a relaxed setting for both business and pleasure entertaining.

For more information about our full facilities and services contact:

Mr Michael Thompson
General Manager
Bay Tree Hotel
Burford
Oxon OX8 4LW
Tel: (0993) 823137 (See Page 27)

AT THE BOTTOM OF A WINDING LANE STANDS . . . THE RED LION

THE RED LION, BLEWBURY.

This charming pub is tucked away in the beautiful village of Blewbury, just off the A417 Reading to Wantage road. At the bottom of a winding lane stands the old-style pub, selling traditional beers from Brakspear. A wide variety of food is served between 12 noon and 10.00 pm, as well as morning coffee and afternoon teas. If you are lucky enough to be there when the pub is empty (or unlucky, depending on your disposition) you will be priveleged to hear the two 'railway' clocks chime, as there is neither piped music nor fruit machines. The large fire is warming in the winter, and the garden is delightful in the warmer months. The bar is beamed and there is a separate restaurant,

and a car park is provided at the rear. Add to all this a warm welcome, and it is obvious why this public house is loyally and locally patronised.

Roger and Caroline Smith are among the few publicans who have so far taken full advantage of the relaxation of the archaic licensing laws. Here at the Red Lion the doors are open from 11am till 11pm, and how pleasant it can be sitting in a cosy pub on a bleak winter's afternoon, or a hot summer's afternoon, when most of the clientele have gone, either sipping a pint, or drinking tea or coffee. The British pub is gradually changing to accommodate the change in people's life-styles, and yet should anyone worry that the character of pubs will be lost forever, they should simply visit the Red Lion to be reassured.

THE WELCOMING INTERIOR OF THE RED LION

THE DELIGHTFUL GARDEN

LANTERN COTTAGE TEA ROOMS, BLEWBURY

BLEWBURY

A large village that nestles below the Berkshire Downs, shaped in a square with a brook dividing it in two. Mentioned in the Domesday Book, Blewbury has many thatched or tiled timbered buildings , old cob walls and four pubs, although in the 19th century there were more. To the south of the village, in the summer months during the First World World War, troops practised on the Churn Down rifle ranges.

Population: 1,452. Map Ref: F 12.

CHURCH
St Michael
A lovely parish church with wide aisles and a long nave. The chancel and transepts are Norman, and the tower was replaced in the 15th century. There is a medieval door and a black letter Bible displayed in the aisle.

PUBLIC HOUSES
The Barley Mow
London Road. Tel: (0235) 850296
The Blue Berry Inn
London Road. Tel: (0235) 850496
The Load of Mischief
South Street. Tel: (0235) 850281
The Red Lion
Nottingham Fee. Tel: (0235) 850403
Old oak-beamed quiet village pub - no music or machines - where 'the customer is King'. Log fires in the winter.
Brewery: Brakspear. Licensee: Roger & Caroline Smith. Opening Hours: 11am-11pm Mon-Sat. Sunday: 12-3pm, 7-10.30pm. Food Available: 12-10pm Mon-Sat.Trad Sunday lunch 12-2pm cold 7-10.30pm. Restaurant Specialities: Homemade specials lunchtime & evenings. Steaks, vegetarian. Garden. Children allowed in the garden.Recommendations: Good Pub Guide.

TEA ROOMS
Lantern Cottage
South Street. Tel: (0235) 850378

OTHER AMENITIES
ART GALLERY
Borlase Gallery
South Street. OX11 9PX Tel: (0235) 850274
Art Gallery and Craft Shop
Months Open: All Year. Days Open: Wednesday to Sunday inclusive. Hours Open: 10 am - 12.30 pm and 2.30pm - 7 pm. Art exhibitions which change every month. Shop selling crafts, pottery, jewelery, wood ware, hand knitwear. Proprietor: Mary Ritchie.

❧ ❧ ❧ ❧ ❧ ❧ ❧

BLOXHAM

A large well-kept village with winding lanes, orange-coloured ironstone houses and thatched cottages. Bloxham enjoyed prosperity in the Middle Ages due to its proximity to Chipping Norton and the wool-producing Cotswolds. A Victorian Gothic school was built in 1860 and dominates the Banbury end of Bloxham. Because the old streets and houses are built so close together, there is little room for modern additions, and so the town retains its charming character.

Population: 2,649. Early closing: Monday/Wednesday. Map Ref: E 3.

PLACES OF INTEREST
Bloxham Village Museum
The Court House.
Tel: (0295) 720283
A museum of local history showing life in Bloxham in earlier eras.
Months Open: All Year. Days Open: Ring for information.

CHURCHES
Baptist Chapel
Methodist Chapel
St Mary
Features a remarkable 14th century spire almost 200 ft high. There are interesting carvings of the Last Judgement by the West door. Inside can be found impressive 13th century arches and medieval carvings. The Victorian east window is the work of William Morris and Burne-Jones. Eton College is the patron of the church and acquired it in 1547 after Godstow Abbey was dissolved.

HOTEL
The Old School & Manor Hotel
Church Street. OX15 4ET Tel: (0295) 720369

GUEST HOUSE
Knoll Guest House
Little Bridge Road. Tel: (0295) 720843

Months Open: All year. Number of Bedrooms: 5. (2 with bathroom). B&B per person: £15. TV. Car park. Garden.

RESTAURANT
The Old Schoolhouse Restaurant
Church St. Tel: (0295) 720369

Classical French Haute Cuisine. Specialities: Salmon Adrienne. Various main course flambés. Hours Open: Lunch: 12-2.30pm. Tea: 3-6pm. Dinner: 7pm. Last Orders: 9.30pm. Closed 5-7pm daily. Open Sundays. Lunch: £ 9.50. Dinner: £ 13.50. House Wine: £ 7.75. Credit Cards: AC. AM. D. V. Seating Capacity: 60. Outside eating. Veg. W/chair. Banquets. Parties. Weddings. Recommendations: AA**RAC **.

PUBLIC HOUSES
The Elephant & Castle
Tel: (0295) 720383
Recommendations: Good Pub Guide.
The Hawk & Partridge
Hawk Lane. Tel: (0295) 720498
The Joiners Arms
Old Bridge Road. Tel: (0295) 720223
The Red Lion
High Street. Tel: (0295) 720352
Free House. Licensee: Mr P. Cooper. Opening Hours: 11 - 2.30pm   7 - 11pm Sundays 12 - 3pm   7 - 10.30pm. Food Available: 12 - 2pm   7 - 10pm.

OTHER AMENITIES
STORE
Virginia House
Tel: (0295) 720596
GARDEN CENTRE
Ridgeway Nurseries
The Ridgeway. Tel: (0295) 720859

🐾 🐾 🐾 🐾 🐾 🐾 🐾

BOARS HILL
Set in the wooded Cumnor Hills south-west of Oxford, Boars Hill affords views of those famous 'dreaming spires', and is heavily associated with the victorian poet Matthew Arnold, who loved the area, and was inspired to write 'The Scholar Gypsy'.
Map Ref: E9.

HOTEL
The Foxcombe Lodge Hotel
Fox Lane. OX1 5DP Tel: (0865) 730746
A family-run hotel with a warm and relaxed atmosphere, set in its own grounds midway between Oxford and Abingdon.

🐾 🐾 🐾 🐾 🐾 🐾 🐾

BODICOTE
This village was the birthplace of John Kersey, the mathematician, in 1616. His most famous work was a treatise on Algebra.
Population: 2,067. Map Ref: F 2.

CHURCHES
Methodist Chapel
St John the Baptist
Only the chancel arch remains of the 13th century building restored in 1844.

PUBLIC HOUSES
The Bakers Arms
Tel: (0295) 3230
Licensee: Mr Geoff Payne.
The Plough Inn
Tel: (0295) 62327

OTHER AMENITIES
CAR HIRE/SELF DRIVE
Jay-Bee Motors
Oxford Road. Tel: (0295) 67557

🐾 🐾 🐾 🐾 🐾 🐾 🐾

BOTLEY
A suburb of Oxford.
Map Ref: F 8.

CHURCH
Botley Baptist Church
Westminster Way. Tel: (0865) 248163

GUEST HOUSES
Gables Guest House
6 Cumnor Hill. Tel: (0865) 862153
A warm welcome awaits you at this modern guest house. Two miles to city centre, direct route for Cotswolds, London, Windsor. Tea/coffee in all rooms.
Months Open: All year. Number of Bedrooms: 5. (2 with bathroom). B&B per person: £12-£15.50. TV. Pets. Car park.
Tilbury Lodge Private Hotel
5 Tilbury Lane. OX2 9NB. Tel: (0865) 864113
Months Open: All year. Number of Bedrooms: 8. (8 with bathroom). B&B per person: £21. TV. Car park. Garden.

RESTAURANTS
The Bilash Tandoori Restaurant
23 Chapel Way. Tel: (0865) 722527
Tong San
20 The Square. Tel: (0865) 248230
Cantonese & Peking Cuisine. Hours Open: Lunch: 12.00pm. Dinner: 6.00pm. Last Orders: 11.45pm. Closed Christmas and

Boxing Day. Open Sundays. Credit Cards: AC. AM. D. V.
Seating Capacity: 70. Banquets. Parties. Weddings.

PUBLIC HOUSES
The Fair Rosamund
Elms Rise. Tel: (0865) 243376
The Seacourt Bridge Inn
Tel: (0865) 243636

OTHER AMENITIES
STORE
Habitat Designs
Seacourt Tower, Westway. Tel: (0865) 790313

🐦 🐦 🐦 🐦 🐦 🐦 🐦

BRIGHTWELL BALDWIN
Brightwell Park dominates the west of this pretty tree-ringed village. The manor house has been demolished, leaving the gates and walls standing; the 17th century dovecote is built in the shape of a Greek cross.
Population: 175. Map Ref: I 11.

PUBLIC HOUSE
Lord Nelson Inn
OX9 5NP Tel: (049161) 2497
Recommendations: Good Pub Guide.

🐦 🐦 🐦 🐦 🐦 🐦 🐦

BRIGHTWELL-CUM-SOTWELL
Tucked away in a loop off the Wallingford to Didcot road, this village consists of two villages joined together, and has some pretty houses between the moated manor house and the Priory.
Population: 1,464. Map Ref: H 11.

RESTAURANT
The Berrick Restaurant
High Street. Tel: (0491) 38077

PUBLIC HOUSE
The Red Lion Public House
Tel: (0491) 37373

🐦 🐦 🐦 🐦 🐦 🐦 🐦

BRILL
A lovely isolated village that stands 700 ft above the Vale of Aylesbury with two greens fringed with charming cottages. Brill windmill dates from 1680, and is one of the oldest to have survived.
Map Ref: I 7.

PLACES OF INTEREST
Brill Windmill
Built in 1680, this windmill was in use until quite recently.
Months Open: Easter - September. Days Open: Sunday. Hours Open: 2.30 - 5. Bank Holidays: Closed.

🐦 🐦 🐦 🐦 🐦 🐦 🐦

BRITWELL SALOME
The name of this little village comes from 'bright well', referring to the spring water, and Sulehame, which was the family name of the owners of the manor in 1236.
Map Ref: I 11.

PUBLIC HOUSE
The Red Lion
Tel: (049161) 2304

🐦 🐦 🐦 🐦 🐦 🐦 🐦

BRIZE NORTON
Dominated by the RAF airbase, the village itself has managed to retain some of its character.
Population: 1,620. Map Ref: B 8.

CHURCH
St Britius

🐦 🐦 🐦 🐦 🐦 🐦 🐦

BROADWELL
A pretty village of stone houses situated on the flat expanse of West Oxford, with an unusually large Norman church, and an inn.
Population: 132. Map Ref: A9.

CHURCH
St Peter & St Paul

PUBLIC HOUSE
The Five Bells
Tel: (036 786) 237

🐦 🐦 🐦 🐦 🐦 🐦 🐦

BROUGHTON
A small ironstone village with a castle, hidden from view behind trees, on the village edge.
Population: 327. Map Ref: E 2.

PLACES OF INTEREST
Broughton Castle
Tel: (0295) 62624

BROUGHTON CASTLE VIEWED FROM THE SOUTH WEST

Built by John de Broughton in 1300 as a manor house and later bought by William of Wykeham, founder of New College Oxford, in 1377. It stands picturesquely on an island within a moat. The manor came into the possession of Sir William Fiennes, second Lord Saye and Sele, in 1450 and has remained in that family ever since. Richard Fiennes remodelled the house in 1554 leaving some medieval vaulted rooms and a private chapel. The eighth Lord Saye and Sele was known as 'Old Subtlety' because of his devious nature during and after the Civil War. The oak drawing room has wonderful panelling and a superb interior porch. Broughton Castle is the finest and most complete medieval house in the county. It is open to the public during the summer.

Months Open: 18 May - 14 September. Days Open: Wednesdays and Sundays, also Thursdays in July and August. Hours Open: 2pm-5pm.

CHURCH
St Mary
14th century church contains various tombs and memorials. Probably built by a de Broughton.

PUBLIC HOUSE
The Saye & Sele Arms
Tel: (0295) 3348

ൠ ൠ ൠ ൠ ൠ ൠ ൠ

BUCKNELL
An old stone village northwest of Bicester, with an old manor house.
Map Ref: H 5.

CHURCH
St Peter
This church has a Norman tower, but was remodelled in the 13th century .

PUBLIC HOUSE
The Trigger Pond
Tel: (0869) 252817

ൠ ൠ ൠ ൠ ൠ ൠ ൠ

BURFORD
Known as 'the gateway to the Cotswolds', Burford is situated in a beautiful stretch of the Windrush valley, near the Gloucestershire border. Most of the houses are made of golden coloured stone, and include a gabled 16th century Court House, now Tolsey Museum, which contains maces, seals and documents of the old corporation. Burford Priory was at one time an Augustinian Hospice, later owned by the Speaker of the Long Parliament of Charles I. It was reduced in size in the 19th century, and is now again a monastic house for nuns. St John the Baptist church is at the bottom of the hill, past some medieval almshouses. Burford throngs with visitors many months of the year, and has become a centre for the antiques trade. There are appealing tea rooms and inns. The

Tourist Information Centre is in the Wadworth Brewery in Sheep Street, which also houses the long established magazine 'The Countryman'.

Population: 1,167. Early closing: Wednesday. Map Ref: A 7.

PLACES OF INTEREST

Burford Garden Centre
Shilton Road.
Tel: (099382) 3117
Contains a working craft centre, a coffee shop and an adventure playground. Cotswold knitwear for sale.
Months Open: All Year. Days Open: Daily. Hours Open: 9-6.

Cotswold Farm Park
Tel: (099382) 3006
120 acres of parkland, a unique survival centre for rare historic breeds of British farm animals, separated from visitors by ditches. There is also a butterfly house (with the largest butterfly cage in the world),an aquarium, a narrow gauge railway and adventure playground.
Months Open: All Year. Days Open: Daily. Hours Open: 10-6 (or dusk).

The Windrush Valley
The gentle River Windrush passes picturesque villages, water meadows, willows and stonewalled farms.

Tolsey Museum
High Street.
Tel: (Secretary) (036781) 294
Museum of Burford's history situated in the old toll-house.
Months Open: Easter-October. Days Open: Daily. Hours Open: 2.30-5.30.

CHURCHES

Baptist Chapel
Witney Street.

Friends Meeting House
Bitt's Lane.

St John the Baptist
Originally built in the 12th century, consists of an impressive Norman tower with an 180ft spire which was added on in the early 15th century. Due to prosperity mainly from wool,the population grew and further aisles and chapels were added to the church to accomodate the church goers, giving the church a complicated interior. Various monuments are found within the church including the Harman monument of 1569 which depicts the earliest Americans commemorated anywhere in England. The church was restored in Victorian times.

St Mary
Tel: (099382) 3200

Wesleyan Chapel

HOTELS

Andrews Hotel
High Street. OX8 4RJ Tel: (099 382) 3151

The Bay Tree Hotel
Sheep Street. OX8 4LW Tel: (099 382) 3137

The Bull Hotel
High Street. OX8 4RH Tel: (099 382) 2220
Centrally located medieval Coaching Inn.

The Cotswold Gateway
Cheltenham Road. OX8 4HX Tel: (099 382) 2148
Modest tourist hotel.

The Golden Pheasant Hotel
High Street. OX8 4RJ Tel: (099 382) 3223

The Highway Hotel
High Street. 0X8 4RG Tel: (099 382) 2136

The Lamb Inn
OX8 5TW Tel: (099 382) 3155

The Winters Tale Hotel
Oxford Road. OX8 4PH Tel: (099 382) 3176
Cosy Cotswold Hotel, adjoining golf course.

RESTAURANT

The Dragon Inn
152 High Street.
Tel: (099 382) 2183
Cantonese & Peking Cuisine. Hours Open: Lunch: 12am. Tea: 6 pm. Dinner: -11pm. Closed Christmas and Boxing Day. Open Sundays. House Wine: £ 6.00. Credit Cards: AC. AM. V. Seating Capacity: 80. Banquet. Parties. Weddings.

BURFORD PRIORY

BURFORD VIEWED FROM FULBROOK HILL

PUBLIC HOUSES

The Lamb Inn
Tel: (099382) 3155
Recommendations: Good Pub Guide.
The Masons Arms
Witney Street. Tel: (099382) 2438
The Mermaid
High Street. Tel: (099382) 2193
The Ox
Rose Hill. Tel: (0865) 778450

TEA ROOMS

Huffkins
High Street. Tel: (099382) 2126
Jackie's Tearooms
High Street. Tel: (099382) 3064
Priory Tea Rooms
37 High Street. Tel: (099382) 3249

OTHER AMENITIES

ART GALLERIES
Brian Sinfield Gallery
The Studio, High Street. Tel: (099382) 2402
Months Open: By Appointment only. Early British & Victorian watercolours; Edwardian, 20th century & modern paintings.
Burford Gallery
Classica House, High Street. Tel: (099382) 2305
19th and 20th century watercolours
Months Open: All year round. Days Open: Monday to Saturday. Hours Open: 9.30am - 6 .00pm. British and continental watercolours and drawings 1770 to the present day. Proprietor: Brian Etheridge.
Stone Gallery
High Street. Tel: (099382) 3302

HOLIDAY ACCOMODATION
Ian Mearns Holidays in France
Priory Lane. Tel: (099382) 3520
Mill at Burford
The Mill. Tel: (099382) 2379
TOURIST OFFICE
Burford Tourist Info Centre
The Old Brewery, Sheep Street. Tel: (099382) 3558
WILDLIFE PARK
Cotswold Wild Life Park
Bradwell Grove. Tel: (099382) 3006

🐾 🐾 🐾 🐾 🐾 🐾 🐾

BUSCOT

A parish on the River Thames, on the border with Gloucestershire, largely built in the same elegant style by the Henderson family who owned Buscot Park. Buscot was famous for cheese in the 18th century; one Edward Loveden collected large quantities of cheese from the surrounding countryside, stored it at Buscot wharf and shipped it annually down the Thames to London.
Population: 172. Map Ref: A 10.

PLACES OF INTEREST

Buscot Park
Tel: (0367) 20786
Built in 1780 this Adam-style house contains the Faringdon Collection of paintings and furniture. Landscaped park and water gardens.
Months Open: April - September. Days Open: Wednesday - Friday, 2nd & 4th Saturday & Sunday in the month. Hours Open: 2-6pm. Easter Saturday & Sunday 2-6pm.

ABOVE: BURFORD PRIORY.   BELOW: A COTSWOLD HOUSE,HIGH STREET, BURFORD

CARTERTON

Named after a Mr Carter, who bought 750 acres of farmland from the Duke of Marlborough before the First World War with the idea of creating a self-sufficient community. Carterton's proximity to RAF Brize Norton is largely responsible for its current population. There is a bustling market on Thursdays.

Population: 11,138. Market day: Thursday. Early closing: Wednesday. Map Ref: B 8.

CHURCH
St John's Church
Burford Road. Tel: (0993) 842249

GUEST HOUSE
Manor Guest House
45 Lawton Avenue. Tel: (0993) 843604

RESTAURANT
The Sharmiana
7 Falkland House, Black Bourton Road. Tel: (0993) 842672

PUBLIC HOUSES
The Beehive Inn
Tel: (0993) 842328
The Osprey
Upavon Way. Tel: (0993) 842788

OTHER AMENITIES
CAR HIRE
Cotswold Limousine Service
14, Burford Road. OX8 3AA Tel: (0993) 842890
SPORTS CLUBS
Carterton Squash Club
Swinbrook Road. Tel: (0993) 84296
Carterton Town F C Social Club
Kilkeeny Lane, Swinbrook Road. Tel: (0993) 824410

🐾 🐾 🐾 🐾 🐾 🐾 🐾

CASSINGTON

Situated five miles from Oxford, where the Evenlode river joins the Thames. There are some houses and a pub around a green.

Population: 649. Map Ref: E 7.

CHURCH
St Peter
Norman church with pre-Reformation pews and a 14th century spire.

PUBLIC HOUSE
Chequers
Tel: (0865) 881380

OTHER AMENITIES
CARAVAN PARK
Cassington Mill Caravan Park
Eynsham Road. OX8 1DB Tel: (0865) 881081
Caravan and Camping Park
Months Open: April 1st - October 31st. Hours Open: 9.00 am - 9.00 pm. Secluded site on banks of river Evenlode. Close to Cotswolds, Oxford, Blenheim Place, Sir Winston Churchill's grave. Fishing permits. Rates: £4.50 tent/caravan/car two persons. Proprietor: R Partridge.
GARDEN CENTRE
Cassington Nurseries
Yarnton Road. Tel: (0865) 882550

🐾 🐾 🐾 🐾 🐾 🐾 🐾

CHACOMBE

Map Ref: F 2.

RESTAURANT
The Cherwell Edge Restaurant
Cherwell Edge Golf Course. Tel: (0295) 712067

PUBLIC HOUSE
The George & Dragon
Silver Street. Tel: (0295) 710602

OTHER AMENITIES
GOLF CLUB
Cherwell Edge GC
Tel: (0295) 711591

🐾 🐾 🐾 🐾 🐾 🐾 🐾

CHADLINGTON

Pretty elongated village of Cotswold stone in the Evenlode valley reputedly the home of St Chad. There are stone cottages and an old picturesque manor house and a medieval church, which was restored inside in the 19th century. The proximity of the Cotswold Wildlife Park and the Forest of Wychwood make this an ideal centre for walking.

Map Ref: C 5.

CHURCH
St Nicholas

HOTEL
Chadlington House Hotel
OX7 3LZ Tel: (060 876) 437
Quiet Country House Hotel with a warm welcome, good food and ideally placed for touring the area.

CHURCH OF ST MARY, CHARLBURY

BEDROOMS: 2 Single, (2 en suite, 2 TV, 2 tea/coffee) `B&B
£ 27.50 - £ 37.50. 7 Double, (7 en suite, 7 TV, 7 tea/coffee) B&B
£ 38.00 - £ 60.00. 2 Twin, (2 en suite, 2 TV, 2 tea/coffee) B&B
£ 40.00 - £ 65.00. 1 Four Poster, £ 80.00. RESTAURANT:
English Cuisine. Dinner: £ 13.50. House Wine: £ 5.75. Credit
Cards: AC. Recommendations: AA**.
Weekend Breaks: 2 nights: £ 63.00. 3 nights: £ 90.00.

PUBLIC HOUSE
The Tite Inn
Mill End. Tel: (060876) 475

⁂ ⁂ ⁂ ⁂ ⁂ ⁂ ⁂

CHALGROVE
A large and mostly modern village situated in the
middle of the flat land to the west of the Chiltern
ridge. In 1643 the battle of Chalgrove Field took
place here, notable because John Hampden, a Parliamentary leader, was mortally wounded, eventually dying in Thame.
Population: 2,519. Early closing: Wed/Thurs. Map Ref: I 10.

CHURCH
St Mary
The 14th century church has a chancel with medieval wall
paintings.

PUBLIC HOUSE
The Lamb Inn
Tel: (0865) 890295

CHARLBURY
The Cotswold stone houses and farms of this large
village overlook the Evenlode Valley. The manor
was built in Anglo-Saxon times and later owned
by the Benedictines of Eynsham Abbey until the
Dissolution. The railway station was designed by
Brunel and has hardly been changed since it was
built. The Museum in Market Street houses a small
collection of local photographs, and displays the
charters given by King Stephen and Henry II.
Since the 17th century Charlbury has been a Quaker
centre, exemplified by a Friends cemetery and a
Friends Meeting House in Market Street, built in
1779. A popular Street Fair is held every September in the elegant Church Street. Cornbury Park
and Wychwood Forest provide an impressive
backdrop to Charlbury. Cornbury itself is one of
the greatest houses in Oxfordshire, but is private
and hidden by a wood. Although it is partly Tudor
it was enlarged in the early 17th century.
Population: 2,637. Early closing: Wednesday. Map Ref: C 6.

PLACES OF INTEREST
Charlbury Museum
Market Street.
Tel: (0608) 810203
Museum showing crafts and industries of Charlbury.
Months Open: Key available from chemist's opposite.
Ditchley Park
Tel: (060 872) 346
Now an Anglo-American conference centre, this fine 18th

century house was designed by James Gibbs, and set in lovely parkland.

CHURCHES
Baptist Church
Friends Meeting House
Methodist Chapel
St Mary
Large partly Norman church but mostly 13th and 14th century with excellent window tracery. One of its Elizabethan vicars was a translator of the Authorized Version of the Bible.

HOTELS
The Bell at Charlbury
Church Street. OX7 3AP Tel: (0608) 810278
Welcoming 17th century stone built hotel.
The White Hart
Market Square. Tel: (0608) 810391

PUBLIC HOUSES
The Bull Inn
Sheep Street. Tel: (0608) 810313
The Charlbury Tavern
Tel: (0608) 208659

OTHER AMENITIES
CARAVAN PARK
Cotswold View Caravan and Camping Site
Enstone Road. Tel: (0608) 810314
TOURS AND SIGHTS
Cotswold Experience
Thames Garden. OX7 3QH Tel: (0608) 810375
T.C.C.L.
27, Ditchley Road. Tel: (0608) 810578

🐾 🐾 🐾 🐾 🐾 🐾 🐾

CHARLTON ON OTMOOR
One of the five villages on Otmoor. The name Charlton means 'freemen's village' and the villagers fought for ancient grazing rights when the moors were drained, but were defeated by troops.
Population: 372. Map Ref: H 6.

CHURCH
St Mary
A church with a 14th century tower which is a landmark for the flat surrounding countryside.

🐾 🐾 🐾 🐾 🐾 🐾 🐾

CHARNEY BASSETT
Situated in sight of the Downs, this little village has

a 17th century belfry and a manor house which was once a grange for Abingdon Abbey. Charney comes from the word 'church' which was the river's name before it became the River Ock in the Middle Ages. There is a path leading to Cherbury Camp, an Iron Age camp associated with King Canute.
Population: 249. Map Ref: D 10.

CHURCH
St Peter

🐾 🐾 🐾 🐾 🐾 🐾 🐾

CHASTLETON
Stands on a high ridge of the Cotswolds close to the borders of Gloucestershire, Worcestershire and Warwickshire.
Map Ref: B 4.

PLACES OF INTEREST
Chastleton House (Photograph page 38)
Tel: (060874) 355
An attractive Jacobean house built for a Witney wool merchant on land owned by Robert Gatesby (of Gunpowder Plot notoriety). 17th century topiary garden.

CHURCH
St Mary the Virgin
A 12th Century church enlarged in the 14th century.

🐾 🐾 🐾 🐾 🐾 🐾 🐾

CHESTERTON
This stone village has a 13th century church with a chiming clock in the tower. There are a few grassy mounds in a field which are all that remain of a Roman town called Alchester.
Population: 1,108. Map Ref: F 5.

CHURCH
St Marys

RESTAURANT
Woods
Tel: (0869) 241444

PUBLIC HOUSE
The Red Cow
Tel: (0869) 241337

OTHER AMENITIES
GOLF CLUB
Chesterton Country GC
Tel: (0869) 241204

CHILDREY

An attractive village with brick cottages, a village green and a pond. There is a manor house opposite the church where Charles I spent a night in 1644.
Population: 437. Map Ref: C 12.

CHURCH
St Mary
The church is mainly 14th century with a Norman font, some old glass and brasses.

ﾟﾟﾟﾟﾟﾟﾟ

CHILTON

A small village with an old church, unfortunately adversely overshadowed by the Atomic Energy Research Establishment at nearby Harwell.
Population: 963. Map Ref: F 10.

RESTAURANT
The Horse & Jockey Hotel & Restaurant
Tel: (0235) 834376

PUBLIC HOUSE
The Rose & Crown
Tel: (0235) 834249

ﾟﾟﾟﾟﾟﾟﾟ

CHINNOR

This largely modern village is dominated by a cement works that hides a most interesting church.
Population: 5,983. Map Ref: K 10.

CHURCH
St Andrew
St Andrew has a high narrow 13th century structure, and contains a comprehensive collection of brasses and pre-Reformation glass. There is a 600 year old stained glass depicting a variety of bishops and saints.

PUBLIC HOUSES
The Black Boy
Tel: (0844) 51455
The Red Lion
Tel: (0844) 51494
Sir Charles Napier
Spriggs Alley. Tel: (024 026) 3011
Free House. Recommendations: Good Pub Guide.

OTHER AMENITIES
CAR HIRE
MSG Chauffeur Services
11, Foresters. Tel: (0844) 53060

ﾟ

CHIPPING NORTON

At 650 feet above sea level, Chipping Norton is the highest town in Oxfordshire. When the Cotswolds were one giant sheep walk, wool merchants and other traders gathered in this bustling market town. There are many fine examples of 16th and 17th century architecture. The wide market place ('chipping' means market) contains a wide variety of shops, good hotels, restaurants and tea shops, as well as the Town Hall and the Tudor Guildhall. A path through the churchyard leads to a field where there are humps and mounds, all that remain of a Norman motte-and-bailey castle. The reputation of Chipping Norton as a textile centre was established by the Bliss family in the 18th century. The present Bliss Mill dominates a valley below the town and is Victorian Versailles in style.
Population: 5,003. Market day: Wednesday. Early closing: Thursday. Map Ref: C 4.

PLACES OF INTEREST
Chipping Norton Museum
New Street.
Tel: (0608) 3342
Housed in the former Baptist schoolroom, this museum has items of local interest, including some Roman remains.

CHURCHES
Baptist Chapel
New Street.
Holy Trinity (RC)
Methodist Chapel
West Street.
St Mary
This church dominates the town; in 1495 it was completely rebuilt in the Perpendicular style, making it one of the most impressive in the area.

HOTELS
The Crown and Cushion Hotel
High Street . OX7 5AD Tel: (0608) 2533
The Fox Hotel
Market Place. OX7 5DD Tel: (0608) 2658
18th century hotel.
The White Hart Hotel
High Street. OX7 5AD Tel: (0608) 2572

GUEST HOUSES
The Crown and Cushion Guest House
High Street. Tel: (0608) 2926
Highlands
73 Burford Road. Tel: (0608) 3320
Southcombe Guest House
The Bungalow, Southcombe. Tel: (0608) 3068

THE KINGS ARMS, CHIPPING NORTON

RESTAURANTS

The Anarkali Restaurant
6 West Street. Tel: (0608) 2785
The Happy Eater
Tel: (0608) 2774
La Madonette
7 Horse Fair. OX7 5AL Tel: (0608) 2320
Little Chef
A361 Roundabout . Tel: (0608) 3307
The Market House Restaurant
4 Middle Row. Tel: (0608) 2781
The Old Bakehouse
50 West Street. Tel: (0608) 3441
The Peking Inn
3 Market Street. Tel: (0608) 2613
Cantonese and Peking Cuisine. Last Orders: 11pm. Closed
Tuesday. Open Sundays. Veg. Banquets. Parties. Weddings.

PUBLIC HOUSES

The Albion Tavern
Burford Road. Tel: (0608) 2860
The Bell Inn
West Street. Tel: (0608) 2521
The Blue Boar Hotel
Goddards Lane. Tel: (0608) 3525
The Bunch of Grapes
Middle Row. Tel: (0608) 2600
Chequers
Goddard Lane. Tel: (0608) 2152
The Kings Arms
18 West Street. OX7 5AA Tel: (0608) 2668
Character Cotswold stone building. Oak beams, large
comfortable rooms.
Brewery: Charrington. Licensees: Doreen & Norman Hoppitt.
Opening Hours: 11 am - 2.30pm. 6.00 pm - 11.00pm. Sundays
12.00am - 3.00pm. 7.00pm - 10.30pm. Restaurant Specialities:
Home cooked food. 4 Bedrooms: B&B per person: £20 single, £30
double.
Oxford House Inn
18 Horse Fair. Tel: (0608) 2918

The Red Lion
Albion Street. Tel: (0608) 41520
The Wagon & Horses
16 London Road. OX7 5AX Tel: (0608) 3369

OTHER AMENITIES
CAR HIRE
A1 Chauffeured Services
High Street. Tel: (0608) 2533
GARDEN CENTRE
Hardy Plants
Banbury Road. Tel: (0608) 41642
HOSPITAL
Chipping Norton War Memorial Hospital
Tel: (0608) 2316
SPORTS CLUBS
Chipping Norton Bowls Club
Greystones. Tel: (0608) 44154
Chipping Norton Football Club Supporters
Hailey Road. Tel: (0608) 2562
THEATRE
Chipping Norton Theatre
2, Spring Street. Tel: (0608) 2350
TOURIST OFFICE
Chipping Norton Tourist Info Centre
New Street Car Park, New Street. Tel: (0608) 44379
WINE BAR
Planters
9, Middle Row. Tel: (0608) 3363

🐾 🐾 🐾 🐾 🐾 🐾 🐾

CHISLEHAMPTON
An obelisk, just outside this small village, marks
the spot of the famous Battle of Chalgrove Field, in
the Civil War.
Map Ref: H 10.

HOTEL
The Coach and Horses
Stadhampton Road. OX9 7UX Tel: (0865) 890255
16th century listed coaching inn with beamed restaurant.

🐾 🐾 🐾 🐾 🐾 🐾 🐾

CHRISTMAS COMMON
A scattered small hamlet that sits in the Chilterns
high above Watlington.
Map Ref: J 11.

PUBLIC HOUSE
The Fox & Hounds
Tel: (049161) 2599
Recommendations: Good Pub Guide.

CHURCH HANBOROUGH

Made up of a small group of stone houses, a church and an inn.
Map Ref: D 7.

CHURCH
St Peter & St Paul
The church has a Norman tympanum showing St Peter with his keys . The nave was completely rebuilt in 1400 with thin columns and an elegant spire which is a landmark in the Evenlode valley.

PUBLIC HOUSE
The Hand & Shears
Tel: (0993) 881394

A traditional country pub with a touch of elegance.
Free house. Licensee: Mr Steve Winstone. Opening Hours: 11 am - 2.30 pm 7pm - 12.00 midnight. Food Available: All day. Restaurant Specialities: Party menus. Full à la carte specials.

🍺 🍺 🍺 🍺 🍺 🍺 🍺

CHURCHILL

Warren Hastings who became the first Governor-General of India was born in one of the stone houses in this quiet village in 1731. William Smith, who produced the first geological map of England, using fossils to ascertain the age of rock strata, was also born in Churchill.
Population: 421. Map Ref: B 5.

CHURCHES
All Saints
The church sits on a hill top, its fine tower (a smaller replica of Magdalen College, Oxford) can be seen for miles, so the town is aptly named.

HOTEL
The Chequers Inn
OX7 6NJ Tel: (060 871) 309

🍺 🍺 🍺 🍺 🍺 🍺 🍺

CLANFIELD

The moated Friars Court stands on the site of a Knights Templar hospice building near this pretty village, with a green and a roadside stream running the whole length of the village. The 12th Century Radcot Bridge and Newbridge, less than two miles away, are regarded as being the oldest on the Thames. There is a disused railway that used to go from Witney to Fairford.
Population: 821. Map Ref: B 9.

CHURCH
St Stephen
The church has a statue of St Stephen halfway up the tower, which depicts him holding a pile of stones, to symbolise his martyrdom.

HOTEL
The Plough at Clanfield
Bourton Road. OX8 2RB Tel: (036 781) 222
A luxury refurbished 16th century Elizabethan manor.
BEDROOMS: 6 Double(6 TV, 6 phone) B&B £ 66.00 - £ 105.00. RESTAURANT: Modern Cuisine. Lunch: £ 11.95. Tea: £ 1.65. Dinner: £ 20.95. House Wine: £ 8.95. Specialities: Game and seafood. Credit Cards: AC. AM. D. V.
Weekend Breaks: 2 nights: £ 93.50. 3 nights: £ 140.25. Allowance towards dinner: £ 15.00.

PUBLIC HOUSE
The Clanfield Tavern
Tel: (036781) 223
Recommendations: Good Pub Guide.

OTHER AMENITIES
BOAT HIRE
Thames Cruises
5, Bourton Close. OX8 2RU Tel: (036781) 313

🍺 🍺 🍺 🍺 🍺 🍺 🍺

CLAYDON

The most northern of all villages in Oxfordshire, which is quiet and peaceful. There is a Norman church and the Oxford Canal passes through.
Population: 325. Map Ref: F 0.

PLACES OF INTEREST
Claydon Granary Museum
Butlin Farm.
Tel: (029 589) 258
This museum shows items of farm machinery of the 19th and early 20th century, housed in old farm buildings.

CHURCH
St James

PUBLIC HOUSE
The Sunrising Inn
OX17 1EW Tel: (029589) 393

🍺 🍺 🍺 🍺 🍺 🍺 🍺

CLIFTON HAMPDEN

A small village with timbered thatched cottages, situated on the Thames. The Barley Mow, on the other side of the seven arch bridge (built by Sir George Gilbert Scott), was immortalised by Jerome K.Jerome in 'Three Men in a Boat'.

Population: 611. Map Ref: G 10.

CHURCH
St Michael & All Angels

HOTEL
The Plough Inn
Tel: (086 730) 7811

RESTAURANT
The Barley Mow
Tel: (086 730) 7847

🐚 🐚 🐚 🐚 🐚 🐚 🐚

COMBE

Combe is a small village situated on a steep slope above the Evenlode. Next to the church is Combe house which is partly Tudor. The village green has an inn overlooking it. Next to the railway there is a working steam engine of 1852, and water wheel with workshops and a working blacksmith's forge, which are open to the public at certain times in the summer.

Population: 660. Map Ref: F 3.

PLACES OF INTEREST
Combe Mill
Tel: (08675) 2652
A restored 1852 engine is in use here and works through many weekends through the summer months.
Months Open: Ring for information.

CHURCH
St Laurence
14th century church has wall paintings, a stone pulpit and lovely old glass.

PUBLIC HOUSE
The Cock Inn
Tel: (0993 89) 288

🐚 🐚 🐚 🐚 🐚 🐚 🐚

COTTISFORD

This small village is built around a ford over a stream, and has a simple small 13th century church and a very interesting manor farmhouse built in the 14th century, which makes it one of the oldest houses in the county. Henry VI gave the Manor to his new college at Eton in the 15th century. The early Georgian stone Cottisford House next to the church was originally built for an Eton tenant. A particularly beautiful road goes through the plantations and the trees of Shelswell Park towards Mixbury.

Population: 167. Map Ref: H 4.

CHURCH
St Mary
Small Early English church which underwent a thorough restoration in 1861.

🐚 🐚 🐚 🐚 🐚 🐚 🐚

COWLEY

A village whose history goes back to the 12th century, when the Augustinians from the Osney Abbey encouraged the building of the church, some parts of which are Norman, although much of it was restored in 1862-5 by GE Street.

Map Ref: G 9.

CHURCH
St James
Beauchamp Lane.

HOTEL
The Original Swan Hotel
OX4 2LF Tel: (0865) 778888

PUBLIC HOUSES
The Cricketers Arms
Temple Road. Tel: (0865) 779358
Exeter Hall
Oxford Road . Tel: (0865) 779127
The Marsh Harrier
40 Marsh Road. Tel: (0865) 775937
The Queens Arms
Churchill Road. Tel: (0865) 774082

OTHER AMENITIES
CAR HIRE
A B C Taxis
70a, Hollow Way. Tel: (0865) 770681
Taxi Firm
Months Open: All year. Days Open: All week. Hours Open: 24 hours per day. Open Bank Holidays.
Dontax
41a, Littlemore Road. Tel: (0865) 779084
CAR HIRE/SELF DRIVE
Whites Cars

138, Hollow Way. Tel: (0865) 777007
STORES
Oxford & Swindon Co-Operative Society Ltd
21, The Square. Tel: (0865) 772221
Woolworths plc
3, The Square. Tel: (0865) 778884
GARDEN CENTRE
New Cowley Garden Centre
81, Wilkins Road. Tel: (0865) 770456
HEALTH CLUB
Temple Club
109, Oxford Road. Tel: (0865) 779115
RAILWAY STATION
Cowley Freight Terminal Ltd
Watlington Road. Tel: (0865) 713900
SNOOKER CENTRE
Temple Club
109, Oxford Road. Tel: (0865) 779115
SPORTS CLUBS
Florence Park Bowls Club
Cornwallis Road. Tel: (0865) 779329
Oxfordshire F A
3, Wilkins Road. Tel: (0865) 775432
SWIMMING POOL
Temple Cowley Swimming Pool
Temple Road. Tel: (0865) 716667
THEATRE
Oxfordshire Touring Theatre Co
TVEI Centre, Cricket Road. Tel: (0865) 778119

🐦 🐦 🐦 🐦 🐦 🐦 🐦

CRAWLEY
Population: 143. Map Ref: C 7.

CHURCH
St Peter

HOTEL
The Lamb Inn
Tel: (0993) 703753

PUBLIC HOUSE
The New Inn
Tel: (0993) 705165

🐦 🐦 🐦 🐦 🐦 🐦 🐦

CROPREDY
A small and interesting village situated four miles due north of Banbury on the River Cherwell. An ancient bridge was built in 1312 across the river, and this is where the Royalists had a major battle triumph when the Parliamentary troops were

beaten back over the bridge and their guns captured. The paths alongside the river are very pleasant for walking.
Population: 652. Map Ref: F 1.

PLACES OF INTEREST
Cropredy Bridge
The site of the Civil War battle of 1644 won by Royalists, which made it something of a unique event.

CHURCH
St Mary
A 14th century ironstone church has a number of interesting memorials, including one to the writer Richard Crossman who lived in the area. The pre-Reformation brass lectern is magnificent and escaped the Puritans by being hidden in the river.

PUBLIC HOUSE
The Brasenose Arms
Tel: (0295) 750244

🐦 🐦 🐦 🐦 🐦 🐦 🐦

CROUGHTON
Stands on the Oxford/Northants border and hosts an American Air Force base. In the church there are some interesting 13th century wall paintings.
Map Ref: G 3.

PUBLIC HOUSE
The Blackbird Inn
38 High Street. Tel: (0869) 23719

🐦 🐦 🐦 🐦 🐦 🐦 🐦

CROWMARSH GIFFORD
Stands on a busy crossroad on the London to Wallingford road, and the Reading to Oxford road. HQ of the South Oxford District Council.
Map Ref: H 12.

HOTEL
The Bell Inn
Tel: (0491) 35324

🐦 🐦 🐦 🐦 🐦 🐦 🐦

CUDDESDON
On top of a steep hill is the site of the palace where the Bishop of Oxford lived, which unfortunately burnt down in 1960. Anglican clergy are trained at Ripon Theologican College, founded in 1856.
Population: 430. Map Ref: H 9.

CHURCH
All Saints
Once belonged to Abingdon Abbey , built around 1180; the aisles were added late in the 13th century, and further additions were made throughout the years. The view from the churchyard on to the Oxford plains is spectacular.

PUBLIC HOUSE
The Bat & Ball Inn
Tel: (08677) 4379

CUDDINGTON
Map Ref: K 7.

PUBLIC HOUSES
The Crown
Aylesbury Road. Tel: (0884) 292222
The Red Lion
Tel: (0844) 291215

OTHER AMENITIES
HOLIDAY ACCOMODATION
Ridge Barn Farm
Ridgebarn Lane. Tel: (0844) 291281

CULHAM
Reached by an ancient bridge, Culham is centred around a village green with a pub, church and an early Stuart manor.
Population: 408. Map Ref: F 10.

CHURCH
St Paul

PUBLIC HOUSES
The Jolly Porter

CHASTLETON HOUSE

Tel: (0235) 24749
The Lion
Tel: (0235) 20327
The Waggon & Horses
Tel: (0235) 23432

CULWORTH
Site of Culham Court, built in 1770 for one Robert Mitchell.
Map Ref: H 1.

GUEST HOUSE
Paddocks Farm
High Street. Tel: (029 576) 491

CUMNOR
Cumnor Place was once the home of Queen Elizabeth the First's favourite, Robert Dudley, the Earl of Leicester.
Population: 4,189. Map Ref: E 9.

CHURCH
St Michael
In this interesting church there is a life-sized statue of Queen Elizabeth the First, originally erected by the Earl of Leicester in the gardens of Dean Court.

HOTEL
The Cumnor Hotel
76 Abingdon Road. OX2 9QW Tel: (0865) 862216

PUBLIC HOUSES
The Bear & Ragged Staff
Appleton Road. Tel: (0865) 862329
Recommendations: Good Pub Guide.
The Vine Inn
Abingdon Road. Tel: (0865) 862567

OTHER AMENITIES
CAR HIRE/SELF DRIVE
Hartwells Group Contracts
Faringdon Road. Tel: (0865) 863898
CARAVAN PARK
Spring Farm
Faringdon Road. Tel: (0865) 863028

CURBRIDGE
Map Ref: C 8.

PUBLIC HOUSES

The Lord Kitchener
Tel: (0993) 702169

Brewery: Morrells. Licensee: Mr R E Bryan. Opening Hours: 11.30 - 2pm 6.30 -11.30pm. Food Available: Every day except Sunday evening. Special board. Garden. Children's area.

The Merry Horn
Tel: (0993) 702205

ﾋﾉ ﾋﾉ ﾋﾉ ﾋﾉ ﾋﾉ ﾋﾉ ﾋﾉ

CUXHAM

A picture postcard village. Houses lead down to the stream which runs alongside the road through the middle of the village.

Map Ref: I 10.

PUBLIC HOUSE

The Half Moon Inn
Tel: (049161) 2451

ﾋﾉ ﾋﾉ ﾋﾉ ﾋﾉ ﾋﾉ ﾋﾉ ﾋﾉ

DEDDINGTON

Deddington, a large attractive ironstone-housed village with a big market place, was recorded in the Domesday Book as being twice the size of Banbury, but over the years it has declined in importance. Large grassy mounds are all that remain of a large castle, where Piers Gaveston, Edward II's favourite, was imprisoned before he was beheaded in 1312. The church used to have the tallest spire in Oxfordshire, but unfortunately in 1634 it collapsed and was rebuilt some fifty years later, reinforced by buttresses. Leadenporch House was the birthplace of Sir Thomas Pope in 1534, founder of Trinity College, Oxford. Also born in Deddington were Sir William Scroggs, who was alledgedly the worst Lord Chief Justice in history, and Mr Bowler of hat fame.

Population: 1,626. Early closing: Tuesday. Map Ref: F 3.

PLACES OF INTEREST

Deddington Castle
Earthworks are all that remain of this once important 12th century castle.

CHURCHES
Congregational Chapel
New Street.
St Peter & St Paul
Wesleyan Chapel
Church Street.
Wesleyan Reform Chapel

HOTELS

Holcombe Hotel
High Street. OX5 4SL Tel: (0869) 38274

Charming 17th century hotel in rural setting of the Cotswolds. Olde Worlde atmosphere and a restaurant renowned for its excellent food.

BEDROOMS: 2 Single, (2 en suite, 2 TV, 2 phone, 2 tea/coffee) B&B £ 50.00 - £ 70.00. 6 Double, (6 en suite, 6 TV, 6 phone, 6 tea/coffee) B&B £ 65.00 - £ 80.00. 6 Twin, (6 en suite, 6 TV, 6 phone, 6 tea/coffee) B&B £ 65.00 - £ 80.00. 6 Family, (6 en suite, 6 TV, 6 phone, 6 tea/coffee) £ 75.00 - £ 95.00. RESTAURANT: French/English Cuisine. Lunch: £ 13.50. Tea: £ 2.75. Dinner: £16.50. House Wine: £ 8.75. À La Carte: £ 14.00. HOTEL INFORMATION: C. W. B. F. 80 space Car Park. Dogs. N/s. 17th century. Sports Facilities: Golf (nearby). Riding (nearby). Fishing (nearby). Tennis (nearby). Credit Cards: AC. AM. D. V. Recommendations: AA**.

Weekend Breaks: 2 nights: £ 72.00. 3 nights: £ 99.00. Allowance towards dinner: £ 13.50.

Hotel Russell
High Street. OX5 4SP Tel: (0869) 38339

17th century country hotel. Home cooking and a friendly atmosphere.

RESTAURANT

Tiffany's Restaurant
Market Place. OX5 4SE Tel: (0869) 38813

PUBLIC HOUSE

The Crown & Tuns Inn
Tel: (0869) 38343

OTHER AMENITIES

ART GALLERY
Grove Galleries
High Street. Tel: (0869) 38397

ﾋﾉ ﾋﾉ ﾋﾉ ﾋﾉ ﾋﾉ ﾋﾉ ﾋﾉ

DIDCOT

Didcot is dominated by the six cooling towers from the huge power station, a landmark for miles around. It was a sleepy little village until the coming of the Great Western Railway put it firmly on the map, creating a station between Paddington, Bristol and Wales, and with a branch line leading to Oxford and the Midlands. The town is mostly 19th and 20th century and 'Old Didcot' is situated on a hill to the west of the town centre, where there are a couple of old houses and a much restored church. The Great Western Railway society created a working railway museum here which is open to the public. (See over)

Population: 14,078. Map Ref: F 11.

PLACES OF INTEREST

Didcot Power Station

Tel: (0235) 815111

A tour lasting for 1 1/2 hours, plus a film about this most visible landmark.

Months Open: By appointment.

Didcot Railway Centre

Tel: (0235) 817200

A large collection of GWR locomotives, coaches and rolling stock reflecting 100 years of history; other attractions include the original engine shed, turntable, and a recreated period station. Special steaming days are held on the first and last Sundays of each month where rides are given on the steam trains.

Months Open: 13th March - 18th December. Days Open: All Week. Hours Open: Monday - Friday: 11-4 Saturday-Sunday: 11-5. Bank Holidays: B H Monday.

HOTEL

The Prince of Wales Hotel

Station Road. OX11 7NN Tel: (0235) 813207

RESTAURANTS

The Lotus House

106 The Broadway. Tel: (0235) 813729

The Wallingford Arms

The Broadway . Tel: (0235) 812282

PUBLIC HOUSES

Broadways

The Broadway. Tel: (0235) 814924

The Crown

187 Queensway. Tel: (0235) 812541

Rowstock Royal Oak

Park Road. Tel: (0235) 812235

The Sprat

Hagbourne Road. Tel: (0235) 812224

The Wallingford Arms

The Broadway . Tel: (0235) 812282

The Waterwitch

Cockcroft Road. Tel: (0235) 812786

The Wheatsheaf

Wantage Road. Tel: (0235) 812225

TEA ROOMS

The Cup & Saucer

2B Edinburgh Drive. Tel: (0235) 812231

OTHER AMENITIES

CAR HIRE

Rowstock Limousine Service

Rowstock House, Rowstock. Tel: (0235) 834273

Months Open: All year. Days Open: All week. Hours Open: 8 am - 6.00 pm. Open Bank Holidays. Chauffeur-driven Daimler li-

HIGH STREET, DORCHESTER WITH THE ABBEY BEHIND

mousines, Mercedes saloons. Proprietor: Oliver Doogue.

CARAVAN PARK

Didcot Caravans

Cavendish Park. Tel: (0235) 816563

GARDEN CENTRE

Broadway Garden Centre

86a, The Broadway. Tel: (0235) 812015

HEALTH CLUB

Main-Line Gym

Garrick Building, Station Road. Tel: (0235) 815537

HOSPITAL

Didcot Hospital

Wantage Road. Tel: (0235) 813226

LEISURE CENTRE

Didcot Leisure Centre

Mereland Road. Tel: (0235) 811250

RAILWAY STATIONS

Didcot Parcels Office

Tel: (0235) 811109

Didcot Station

Station Road. Tel: (0235) 811115

SNOOKER CENTRE

Broadway Snooker Club

76, Lower Broadway. Tel: (0235) 819921

SPORTS CLUB

Didcot Town F C

Tel: (0235) 813212

THE WAR MEMORIAL, DORCHESTER-ON-THAMES

DORCHESTER-ON-THAMES

This beautiful village, once the Saxon capital of Wessex, is the most historic spot in Oxfordshire. It stands above the confluence of the rivers Thame and Thames, overlooked by the Sinodun Hills. In AD635 the Benedictine monk Birinus, sent from Rome to convert the West Saxons, baptized King Cynegil and his court in the Thame; he then built a church which became the cathedral of Wessex. The Augustinians built the glorious 200 ft abbey that dominates the village. The new by-pass diverts most of the traffic away from the timbered houses, thatched cottages, ancient inns and antique shops, creating a peaceful atmosphere.

Population: 1,008. Early closing: Wednesday. Map Ref: G 11.

PLACES OF INTEREST
Dorchester Abbey Museum
Tel: (0865) 340056
A small museum with history of the Abbey and village.
Months Open: April - September. Days Open: April: Weekends. May-Sept: Tuesdays and Weekends . Hours Open: April: 3-6. May-Sept: 10.30-6. Sundays 2-6 . Bank Holidays: Good Friday, Easter weekend 3-6.

CHURCHES
Abbey of St Peter and St Paul

St Birinus (RC)
Bridge End.

HOTELS
Fleur de Lys Inn
High Street. Tel: (0865) 340502
The George Hotel
High Street. OX9 8HH Tel: (0865) 340404
13th century Coaching Inn, warm informal atmosphere.
The White Hart
26 High Street. OX9 8HN Tel: (0865) 340074

RESTAURANT
Little Chef
Dorchester Road. Tel: (0865) 340829

PUBLIC HOUSE
The Plough Inn
Tel: (0865) 340012

OTHER AMENITIES
ART GALLERY
Dorchester Galleries
Rotten Row. Tel: (0865) 341116

🍎 🍎 🍎 🍎 🍎 🍎

DRAYTON

A small hamlet on the outskirts of Banbury.
Population 239 Map Ref:F2

CHURCH
St Peter

PUBLIC HOUSE
The Roebuck Inn
Tel: (0295) 730542

ᴥ ᴥ ᴥ ᴥ ᴥ ᴥ ᴥ

DRAYTON

A village with a High Street of some character, and an early 14th century church.
Population: 2,040. Map Ref: E 11.

PUBLIC HOUSES
The Red Lion
Tel: (0235) 31381
The Wheatsheaf
The Green. Tel: (0235) 31485
Brewery: Morlands. Licensee: Mr M G Legg. Opening Hours: 11 - 2.30 pm 6 - 11 pm. Food Available: 12 -2 pm 6.30 - 8.30pm. Not Sundays. Garden.

ᴥ ᴥ ᴥ ᴥ ᴥ ᴥ ᴥ

DRAYTON ST LEONARD

A tiny village between the rivers Thame and Thames, with a mixture of old and new houses, a pub, and a church dedicated to St Leonard.
Population: 271. Map Ref: H 10.

CHURCH
St Leonard
This church has an unusual timber-framed tower.

PUBLIC HOUSE
The Three Pigeons
High Street. Tel: (0865) 890217

ᴥ ᴥ ᴥ ᴥ ᴥ ᴥ ᴥ

DUCKLINGTON

Ducklington is a small rural village, south of Witney, with stone houses around a pond, and a church with lovely windows.
Population: 1,234. Map Ref: C 8.

CHURCH
St Bartholomew

PUBLIC HOUSE
The Bell Inn
Tel: (0993) 702514

DUNS TEW

A charming little village, where thatched stone cottages cluster around the 17th century church.
Population: 412. Map Ref: F 4.

CHURCH
St Mary Magdalene
Largely rebuilt in the 19th century, but retains some early features, notably a Norman font.

RESTAURANT
The White Horse Inn & Restaurant
Tel: (0869) 40272

OTHER AMENITIES
GARDEN CENTRE
Goundrey & Son Ltd
Tel: (0869) 40224
HOLIDAY ACCOMODATION
Daisy Hill Farm
R F Moffatt. Tel: (0869) 40293

ᴥ ᴥ ᴥ ᴥ ᴥ ᴥ ᴥ

EAST HAGBOURNE

A pretty village with the main street running alongside a brook, and timber and plaster houses with overhanging top storeys. At one end is the Lower Cross, but a stump is all that remains of an earlier cross, after Cromwell's men wasted it in 1644.
Population: 1,069. Map Ref: F 12.

CHURCH
St Andrew
The church has a 600 year old door and a 12th century chancel arch, and although much of the church was enlarged later, nothing has really changed since 1450.

PUBLIC HOUSES
The Fleur de Lys
Tel: (0235) 813247
The Spread Eagle
Tel: (0235) 813639
The Travellers Inn
Main Road. Tel: (0235) 812391
Brewery: Ushers. Licensee: Mr M D Beesley. Opening Hours: 11am - 2.30pm 6 - 11pm Sunday 12 - 3 pm 7 - 10.30pm . Food Available: everyday except Tuesday lunchtimes.

ᴥ ᴥ ᴥ ᴥ ᴥ ᴥ ᴥ

EAST HANNEY

Many villages situated in the Vale of White Horse are paired, an east with a west. East Hanney, twinned with West Hanney, has windy lanes and timber houses , modern houses and farmyards. There is an old manor house near the brook dated 1710, once owned by Sir William Scroggs, the corrupt Lord Chief of Justice in Charles II's reign. *Population: 759. Map Ref: D 12.*

CHURCH
St James

RESTAURANT
The Vintage Restaurant
Tel: (023587) 287

PUBLIC HOUSE
The Crown Inn
Oxford Road. Tel: (023587) 269

☙ ☙ ☙ ☙ ☙ ☙ ☙

EAST HENDRED

A very picturesque village with many old brick and timber houses. Hendred House is a medieval manor which still belongs to the Eyston family who have owned it since 1450. They are descendants of Sir Thomas More and the house contains relics of More and Bishop John Fisher. *Population: 1,104. Map Ref: E 11.*

CHURCHES
Jesus Chapel
St Augustine of Canterbury
The church features one of the oldest working clocks in England, built in 1525.
St Mary (RC)

GUEST HOUSE
Ridgeway Lodge Guest House
Skeats Bush. Tel: (0235) 833360

PUBLIC HOUSES
The Plough Inn
Tel: (0235) 833213
The Wheatsheaf Inn
Tel: (0235) 833229
Recommendations: Good Pub Guide.

OTHER AMENITIES
FISH FARM
Clearwater Fish Farm
Ludbridge Mill. Tel: (0235) 833732

EAST ILSLEY

Twinned with West Ilsley, these villages are set in the heart of the rolling Berkshire Downs. The two old coaching inns sit side-by-side in the centre of the village, at the old crossroads; the A34 Oxford to Newbury road has now assumed motorway proportions, and by-passes the village, leaving it to its own sleepy devices. *Map Ref: E 13.*

CHURCH
St Mary

HOTELS
The Crown & Horns
High Street. Tel: (063 528) 205
The Swan Hotel
Tel: (063 528) 238

PUBLIC HOUSE
The Star Inn
High Street. Tel: (063 528) 215

☙ ☙ ☙ ☙ ☙ ☙ ☙

EATON

Eaton is a stone cottage hamlet with a charming pub, just north of Appleton. *Map Ref: E 9.*

PUBLIC HOUSE
The Eight Bells Public House
Tel: (0865) 862983
The archetypal English country pub - oak beams, inglenook fireplace, horse brasses, and fine oil paintings. Delightful garden. In quiet secluded hamlet, yet easily reached from all main roads.
Brewery: Morlands. Licensee: Mr Derrick Johns. Opening Hours: 11 am - 3 pm 6.30 - 11 pm. Food Available: 12 - 2 pm 6.30 - 9.30pm. Restaurant Specialities: All À La Carte, plus daily special. Garden.

☙ ☙ ☙ ☙ ☙ ☙ ☙

ENSLOW

Established in 1770 around the wharf of the newly cut Oxford canal. The famous Rock of Gibraltar Inn is here. *Map Ref: F 6.*

PUBLIC HOUSE
The Rock of Gibraltar
Tel: (086 983) 223

☙

THE ALMSHOUSES, EWELME, WITH ST MARY'S IN THE BACKGROUND

ENSTONE

Derived from 'Ennas Stone' there are still some burial stones to be seen here. There is a barn with a stone recording that it was built by the Abbot of Wynchcome in 1382, and it is still in use. The village is on the road from London to Worcester, and has consequently had a lot of traffic passing through it since the 1800's.

Population: 998. Map Ref: D 5.

CHURCH
St Kenelm

The church has a Norman doorway and a Tudor arch.

HOTEL
The Crown Inn

Tel: (060 872) 262

BEDROOMS: 3 Double, (2 en suite, 3 TV, 3 tea/coffee) B&B £ 20.00 - £ 38.00. 1 Twin, (1 en suite, 1 TV, 1 tea/coffee) B&B £ 20.00 - £ 38.00.

Weekend Breaks: 2 nights: £ 45.00.

PUBLIC HOUSE
The Bell Inn

Tel: (060 872) 362

EPWELL

A village with an old mill house, thatched cottages, a ford, a green and an old church.

Population: 224. Map Ref: D 2.

CHURCH
St Anne

PUBLIC HOUSE
The Chandlers Arms

Tel: (029578) 244

EWELME

The name Ewelme comes from an Old English word meaning 'spring, source of river' and the spring in question still runs through the village with watercress beds and trout farms along some of its length. 15th century almshouses, the church, and an old schoolhouse are among some of the brick and flint built cottages that make up this charming village. The church is an excellent example of the Perpendicular style and was built all at one time instead of over centuries like most village churches. There are some famous tombs,

including that of Thomas Chaucer, the poet's son, and the Constable of Wallingford. More recently Ewelme was the setting for the TV serial of John Mortimer's 'Paradise Postponed'.
Population: 514. Map Ref: I 11.

CHURCH
St Mary

PUBLIC HOUSE
The Shepherds Hut
High Street. Tel: (0491) 35661

ᘛ ᘛ ᘛ ᘛ ᘛ ᘛ ᘛ

EYNSHAM
A small town straddling an area between the Thames and the A40, which has become something of a satellite town for nearby Oxford. Belonging to the Anglo-Saxon kings of Mercia in the 8th century AD, Eynsham came into prominence with the building of a Benedictine Abbey in 1000 AD, the remains of which lie in a field near the large church. Nearby is the Swinford Toll Bridge.
Population: 4,339. Map Ref: E 8.

CHURCHES
Catholic Apostle Church
Mill Street.
St Leonard
This church has an impressive 14th century tower, some interesting wall paintings and brasses.
St Peter (RC)

HOTEL
The Swan Hotel
21 Acre End. OX8 1PE Tel: (0865) 881225

RESTAURANTS
The Epicure Restaurant
4 Lombard Street . Tel: (0865) 880777
The Evenlode (Berni Inns)
Tel: (0865) 881215
Little Chef
Jet Garage A40. Tel: (0865) 881696
O'Learys Restaurant
Newland Street. OX8 1LA Tel: (0865) 881384
English Cuisine. Last Orders: 9.30pm. Closed Saturday am, Sunday and Monday pm. Open Sundays. Credit Cards: AC. V. Seating Capacity: 50. Veg. W/chair. Parties. Weddings.

PUBLIC HOUSES
The Jolly Sportsman
Eynsham. Tel: (0865) 881427

The Newlands Inn
Tel: (0865) 881486
The Queens Head
Tel: (0865) 881229
The Red Lion
The Square. Tel: (0865) 882903
The Star Inn
Tel: (0865) 881287
The Talbot Inn
Oxford Road. Tel: (0865) 881348
The White Hart
Newland Street. Tel: (0865) 880711

OTHER AMENITIES
BOAT HIRE
Oxford Cruisers
Cruiser Station. Tel: (0865) 881698
CAR HIRE/SELF DRIVE
Spareacre Hire
Spareacre Lane. Tel: (0865) 881316
Car and Van or Minibus hire
Months Open: All year. Days Open: Monday - Saturday. Hours Open: 8 am - 5.30 pm. Open on all Bank Holidays for return or collection by prior arrangement . Continental travel for all types of vehicles. 12 and 15 seat minibuses for self drive hire. Proprietor: William George Penny.
CARAVAN PARK
Swinford Farm
Eynsham. Tel: (0865) 881368
FISH FARM
Isis Fish Farm
Eynsham Mill. Tel: (0865) 881751

ᘛ ᘛ ᘛ ᘛ ᘛ ᘛ ᘛ

FARINGDON
A largely unspoilt stone-built country town in the Vale of the White Horse. It is at the high point of a limestone ridge, sometimes called the Golden Ridge, that runs from the Wiltshire border to Oxford. Faringdon is a town with various royal connections: King Alfred had a palace here, his son Edward, first King of England, died here, and King John granted the town a charter to hold markets in 1218, which still continue today. Faringdon grew prosperously in the 15th and 16th centuries and saw much action during the Civil War as each side battled for the crossing at Radcot. The 17th century pillared Market Hall is the focal point of the town. It stands in the market place, down the hill from the church, surrounded by Georgian fronted shops and inns. Behind the church is Faringdon House.
Population: 4,787. Market day: Tuesday. Early closing: Monday. Map Ref: B 10.

GREAT COXWELL BARN

ALL SAINTS CHURCH, FARINGDON

PLACES OF INTEREST
Great Coxwell Barn
One of the country's largest monastic stone tithe barns, built by the Cistercian Monks in the 13th century. Preserved by the National Trust.
Months Open: All Year. Days Open: Daily. Hours Open: 9-6. Bank Holidays: Open.

CHURCH
All Saints
This church, which looks down onto the town from a hill, is a Norman and early Norman structure. It lost its spire during the Parliamentary cannonade in 1644, evidence of which can be seen by a cannonball lodged in the east wall.

HOTELS
The Bell Hotel
Market Place. SN7 7HP Tel: (0367) 20534
Old Coaching Inn, pretty bedrooms and good food.
The Faringdon Hotel
Market Place. SN7 7HL Tel: (0367) 20536
Believed to stand on site of Alfred the Great's Castle.
Portwell House
Market Place. SN7 7HU Tel: (0367) 20197

RESTAURANTS
The Rats Castle
1 Bromsgrove. Tel: (0367) 20148
Restaurant 1645
23 Market Place. Tel: (0367) 20678
Sinclairs
6 Market Place. Tel: (0367) 20945

PUBLIC HOUSES
The Bakers Arms
Ferndale Street. Tel: (0367) 20574
The Bull Inn
27 London Street. Tel: (0367) 20306
The Duke of Wellington
27 Lechlade Road. Tel: (0367) 20545
The Queens Arms
40 Coxwell Street. Tel: (0367) 21207

The Red Lion
3 The Cornmarket. Tel: (0367) 20656
The Swan
1 Park Road. Tel: (0367) 22192
The Volunteer Inn
2 Gloucester Street. Tel: (0367) 20407
The Wheatsheaf
London Street. Tel: (0367) 20200

OTHER AMENITIES
GARDEN CENTRE
Radclive Tucker Ltd
Folly Farm, Stanford Road. Tel: (0367) 20053
SPORTS CLUBS
Berks and Bucks Football Association
15a, London Street. Tel: (0367) 22099
Faringdon Town F.C.
Tuckers Park, Park Road. Tel: (0367) 21759

🐎 🐎 🐎 🐎 🐎 🐎 🐎

FAWLEY
A tiny village, grouped with South Fawley, set in the rolling Berkshire Downs. There is a good pub, and the church was restored by GE Street, who must have had a very busy working life.
Map Ref: J 12.

CHURCH
St Mary
A 13th century church restored in 1866, with beautiful views over the Downs. Stained glass window by Morris.

PUBLIC HOUSE
The Walnut Tree
Tel: (049163) 360

🐎 🐎 🐎 🐎 🐎 🐎 🐎

FERNHAM
A small village with some thatched cottages.
Population: 194. Map Ref: A11.

PUBLIC HOUSE
The Woodman Inn
Tel: (0367) 643
Recommendations: Good Pub Guide.

🍺 🍺 🍺 🍺 🍺 🍺 🍺

FEWCOTT
A modern development with a partly Norman church and remains of a small castle.
Map Ref: G4

PUBLIC HOUSE
The White Lion
Fritwell Road. Tel: (08696) 6639

🍺 🍺 🍺 🍺 🍺 🍺 🍺

FILKINS
Close to the Gloucestershire border, one time home of Sir Stafford Cripps, the puritanical Labour Chancellor of the Exchequer. A brook separates Filkins and the village, Broughton Pogges.
Population: 1,140. Map Ref: A 8.

PLACES OF INTEREST
Cotswold Woollen Weavers
Tel: (036786) 491
A working mill with exhibition areas and a mill shop. Coffee shop and picnic area.
Months Open: All Year. Days Open: Daily. Hours Open: Monday-Saturday: 10-6 pm. Sunday: 2-6pm.

CHURCH
St Peter

🍺 🍺 🍺 🍺 🍺 🍺 🍺

FINSTOCK
Situated to the south of the once Royal Forest of Wychwood, this village is a mixture of old cottages and modern bungalows.
Population: 1,521. Map Ref: C 6.

PUBLIC HOUSE
The Plough Inn
Tel: (099386) 333

🍺 🍺 🍺 🍺 🍺 🍺 🍺

FOREST HILL
Old farms and a little church, with buttresses to stop it sliding down the steep slope above the Oxford bypass, make up this little village.
Population: 618. Map Ref: H 8.

CHURCH
St Nicholas
The large bellcote of this church is visible from the A40. There is some interesting 15th century embroidery on the altar. John Milton was married here in 1643; the marriage unfortunately did not endure, and inspired the poet's treatise on divorce.

PUBLIC HOUSES
The Kings Arms
Tel: (08677) 2673
The White Horse Inn
Wheatley Road. Tel: (08677) 3927

🍺 🍺 🍺 🍺 🍺 🍺 🍺

FREELAND
A small village of mixed old and new houses, so named because Freeland started life as a squatters' settlement on the outskirts of Eynsham in the 17th century.
Population: 1,348. Map Ref: D 7.

CHURCH
St Mary

PUBLIC HOUSE
The Oxfordshire Yeoman
Tel: (0993) 882051

OTHER AMENITIES
GARDEN CENTRE
Freeland Nurseries
Wroslyn Road. Tel: (0993) 881430

🍺 🍺 🍺 🍺 🍺 🍺 🍺

FRILFORD
A small village with scattered houses, situated to the west of Abingdon.
Population: 201. Map Ref: E 10.

HOTELS
The Ark
Wantage Road. Tel: (0865) 391911

RESTAURANT
The Fleur De Lys
Cothill. OX13 6JW
Tel: (0865) 390223
Continental Cuisine. Specialities: Dover Sole Casa Reale and Aylesbury Duck in Brandy and Orange Sauce. Hours Open: Lunch: 12-2.00. Dinner: 7 - 10.30. Last Orders: 10.30. Closed

Sunday evenings. Sunday lunch. Lunch: £ 7.50. Dinner: £ 10.50. Credit Cards: AC. AM. V. Seating Capacity: 50. Outdoor eating. Vegetarian. Parties. Weddings.

OTHER AMENITIES

GARDEN CENTRE
Millets Farm Garden Centre
Kingston Road. Tel: (0865) 391923

🐾 🐾 🐾 🐾 🐾 🐾 🐾

FRILFORD HEATH
Map Ref; E10

PUBLIC HOUSE
The Black Horse
Tel: (0865) 390530

🐾 🐾 🐾 🐾 🐾 🐾 🐾

FRINGFORD
A small village centred round some attractive greens, that has been the home of some prominent politicians over the years, most notably Lord Sidmouth, who succeeded Pitt as Prime Minister.
Population: 396. Map Ref: J 4.

CHURCH
St Michael
The church is Norman but has been restored a great deal.

PUBLIC HOUSE
The Butchers Arms
OX6 9EB Tel: (08697) 363
Licensee: Mr John Bellinger.

🐾 🐾 🐾 🐾 🐾 🐾 🐾

FRITWELL
A large grey stone village northwest of Bicester, with a 17th century manor house, which has several unsavoury legends associated with it. One such concerned the two Longueville brothers, who quarrelled over a lady. It resulted in one brother being locked in a dog kennel in the attic by the other, for fourteen years, said to be mad. He probably was by the time he was let out.
Population: 525. Map Ref: G 4.

CHURCH
St Olave
Restored in the 19th century by G E Street, this church is one of the very few in the country dedicated to Olaf of Norway. Possibly Saxon in origin.
🐾

FULBROOK
A small village of stone cottages with a Norman church, in close vicinity to Burford.
Population: 330. Map Ref: A 7.

CHURCH
St James

HOTEL
Elm Farm House Private Hotel
Meadow Lane. OX8 4BW Tel: (099 382) 3611

PUBLIC HOUSES
The Carpenters Arms
Tel: (099382) 3275
The Masons Arms
Tel: (099382) 2354

🐾 🐾 🐾 🐾 🐾 🐾 🐾

FYFIELD
A by-passed village with a 14th century manor house (now the rare book department of Blackwells the Booksellers). The church was rebuilt 100 years ago after being gutted by fire. The White Hart was a 15th century chapel, and is now a hostelry that attracts custom from far and wide.
Population: 450. Map Ref: D 10.

RESTAURANT
The White Hart
Tel: (0865) 390585
Bar Food, À La carte Restaurant . Specialities: Game in season. Hours Open: Lunch: 12 - 2.00pm. Dinner: 7 - 10.00pm. Last Orders: 10.00pm. Bar food only Sundays. House Wine: £ 4.20. Credit Cards: AC. AM. D. V. Seating Capacity: 40/60. Outdoor Eating . Veg. Parties. Recommendations: ER.

🐾 🐾 🐾 🐾 🐾 🐾 🐾

GARSINGTON
Garsington is situated on a steep hill, with a mainly Tudor stone manor house (see front cover) surrounded by yew hedges, once owned by Lady Ottoline Morrell in the '20's. T S Elliot, Virginia Woolf and D H Lawrence were all visitors; Lady Morrell has a memorial in the church. There is an Italianate terraced garden created for her ladyship, that has a long pool with an island in the middle. The current owner is expanding the gardens.
Population: 1,772. Map Ref: G 9.

CHURCH
St Mary

PUBLIC HOUSES

The Plough Inn
Oxford Road. Tel: (086736) 395

The Red Lion
35 Garsington Road. Tel: (086736) 413

The Three Horseshoes
Tel: (086736) 276

OTHER AMENITIES

CAR HIRE
Findlay Cars
106, Oxford Road. Tel: (086736) 598
Chauffeur Driven Car Hire
Months Open: All year. Days Open: All week. Hours Open: 6 am - 12.00 midnight. Open Bank Holidays. Airports and any journey undertaken. Rates: Oxford to Heathrow : £32 plus VAT. Oxford to Central London: £45 plus VAT. Proprietor: J A Findlay.

CARAVAN PARK
King Copse Park
Lower Road. Tel: (0865) 776735

GOOSEY

Derived from the words 'goose island', this village's farms and houses encircle a huge village green. The monks of Abingdon used to fatten geese here for their Abbot's table.
Population: 130. Map Ref: C 11.

PUBLIC HOUSE

The Pound Inn
Tel: (03677) 329

GORING HEATH

Goring Heath covers quite a large area of woodland. Almshouses, founded in 1724 by the Lord Mayor of London, stand back from the road, with an impressive chapel in the centre. There is a picturesque Post Office built around the turn of the century, constructed in part of weather boarding. *Population: 1,281. Map Ref: H 13.*

PUBLIC HOUSE

King Charles Head
Reading Road. Tel: (0491) 680268

GORING-ON-THAMES

A large and pleasant riverside village full of Edwardian buildings and quaint pubs, where the river Thames separates the Chilterns from the Berkshire Downs, through the Goring Gap. The prehistoric Icknield Way crossed the river from Goring to Streatley, where a ferry existed until a bridge was built about 100 years ago.
Population: 3,382. Early closing: Wednesday. Map Ref: H 13.

THE ELEGANT SWEEP OF THE HIGH STREET, GORING-ON-THAMES

ST THOMAS OF CANTERBURY CHURCH, GORING-ON-THAMES

CHURCHES
Our Lady and St John (RC)
St Thomas of Canterbury
There are still traces of the medieval priory in this much-altered Norman church, which stands picturesquely on an inlet off the river.

HOTELS
John Barleycorn Inn
Manor Road. RG8 9DP Tel: (0491) 872509
The Miller of Mansfield
High Street. RG8 9AW Tel: (0491) 872829
Ivy covered Tudor style inn, oak beams and open fires.

PUBLIC HOUSES
The Catherine Wheel
Station Road. RG8 9HB Tel: (0491) 872379
Goring's oldest pub. Real ales. Good food at reasonable prices. Fine wines.
Brewery: Brakspear. Licensee: Mr James Richard Saunders. Opening Hours: 11 - 3 pm 6 - 11 pm. Food Available: 12 - 2pm 7 - 9.30 pm. Specialities: Home made soups. Home made Pies. Grills. Seafood. Garden. Children's Area.
The Magpie
Fairfield Road. Tel: (0491) 872241
The Queens Arms
Reading Road. Tel: (0491) 872825

OTHER AMENITIES

RAILWAY STATION
Goring Station
Gatehampton Road. Tel: (0491) 872822
SAILING CLUB
Goring Thames Sailing Club
18, Summerfield Rise. Tel: (0491) 873681

🐝 🐝 🐝 🐝 🐝 🐝 🐝

GREAT BARRINGTON
Map Ref: A 6.

HOTEL
The Inn for All Seasons
OX8 4TN Tel: (04514) 324
16 C coaching Inn built of Cotswold stone . Comprises log fires, a real ale bar and traditional home cooking. The hotel's extensive gardens have delightful views over Windrush Valley.
BEDROOMS: 5 Double, (5 en suite, 5 TV, 5 phone, 5 tea/coffee) B&B £ 24.50 - £ 35.00. 5 Twin, (5 en suite, 5 TV, 5 phone, 5 tea/coffee) B&B £ 24.50 - £ 35.00.   RESTAURANT: English Cuisine. Lunch: £ 7.50. Dinner: £ 12.75. House Wine: £ 5.95. Specialities: Roasts and grills. HOTEL INFORMATION: CF. W. Sports Facilities: Golf. Riding. Fishing. Credit Cards: AC. AM. D. V. Recommendations: AA***. ER. M. RAC **.
Weekend Breaks: 2 nights: £ 39.00*. 3 nights: £ 37.50*. (*Per night) Allowance towards dinner: £ 12.75.
🐝

GREAT BOURTON

An L-shaped 17th century manor house stands near to the church. Nearby is Friar's Cottage, which has the date 1685 above an oval window.
Map Ref: F 1.

CHURCH
All Saints

PUBLIC HOUSES
The Bell Inn
Tel: (0295) 750504
The Swan Inn
Tel: (0295) 758181
Recommendations: Good Pub Guide.

🍺 🍺 🍺 🍺 🍺 🍺 🍺

GREAT HASELEY

Situated in quiet farmland country, with old thatched cottages and a manor house, church and church farm.
Population: 575. Map Ref: I 9.

CHURCH
St Peter
A large church with a Norman door and a 13th C. chancel. Christopher Wren, father to the architect, was a rector here. Many of the rectors went on to become bishops.

PUBLIC HOUSE
The Plough Inn
Rectory Road. Tel: (084 46) 283
Brewery: Halls Oxford and West. Licensee: Mr Lionel Eric Cook. Opening Hours: 11.30am - 2pm 6.30 - 11pm. Food Available: 12 - 2pm Mon - Sat. Garden. Children's area.

🍺 🍺 🍺 🍺 🍺 🍺 🍺

GREAT MILTON

Situated in the valley of the Thame, Great Milton is an unspoiled village where thatched cottages and two inns encircle the green; there is a world famous French restaurant.
Population: 803. Map Ref: I 9.

CHURCHES
St Mary
During a complete restoration in 1850, evidence of a fire in the 14th century was found.The tomb of Sir Michael Dormer, Lord Mayor of London, who died in 1616, and his wife and father, has a remarkable alabaster carving.On a wall hang two pikes that were issued to the Home Guard in 1940 to help them stop the Nazi invasion!

RESTAURANT
Le Manoir aux Quat ' Saisons (see pages 52-53)
Tel: (0844) 278881
French (The Very Best) Cuisine. Specialities: Pave de Saumon Sauvage Fumé au Manoir; Souffle au Raifort et Beurre de Concombres; Pigeonneau de Norfolk en croute de sel; Trio de chocolats. Hours Open: Lunch: 12.15-2.15pm. Tea: PM. Dinner: 7.15-10.15pm. Last Orders: 10.15pm. Residents only Monday nights. Closed Monday and Tuesday lunchtimes. Open Sundays. Lunch: £ 21.50. Dinner: £ 44.00. House Wine: £ 17.00. Credit Cards: Ac. Am. D. V. Seating Capacity: 65. NS Areas. Vegetarian. Banquets up to 45. Parties up to 45. Weddings. Recommendations: AA *** .ER *** (86%). M **.

PUBLIC HOUSES
The Bell Inn
The Green. Tel:·(0844) 279270
The Bull
Tel: (0844) 279726

🍺 🍺 🍺 🍺 🍺 🍺 🍺

GREAT ROLLRIGHT

Great Rollright and Little Rollright are situated on either side of the Rollright Stones; both are pretty, with interesting churches.
Map Ref: C 3.

PLACES OF INTEREST
Rollright Stones
Three Bronze age monuments comprising the King's Men, a 70 stone circle 100 feet in diameter, 2,000 years old, the Whispering Knights and the King's Stone, an isolated standing stone. Man's presence in the area stretches back to 6000 BC. These interesting stones are off the main roads and very hard to find as there are no signposts at all. We would suggest that you ask for directions in one of the pubs in Great or Little Rollright.
Months Open: All Year. Days Open: Daily. Hours Open: 9-6. Bank Holidays: Open.

CHURCH
ST ANDREW

PUBLIC HOUSE
The Unicorn
High Street. Tel: (0608) 737751

🍺 🍺 🍺 🍺 🍺 🍺 🍺

GREAT TEW

This village in a beautiful tree-lined valley, has ironstone cottages, thatched or with stone tiles. The surrounding woodland looks (Cont. p 54)

LE MANOIR AUX QUAT' SAISONS

IN 1984 THE Manor House at Great Milton came up for sale at auction. It is one of the most beautiful manor houses in the county, so its fate was obviously the concern of many. Manor houses are generally destined to become either old people's homes, conference centres, flats, or the homes of absent super-rich foreigners or all-too-resident pop stars. Sometimes, if fortunate, they are transformed into an hotel and restaurant of international acclaim and repute.

Great Milton Manor became the latter, when it was bought by M. Raymond Blanc, a rising culinary star, who had already established his credentials at a number of restaurants in Oxford.

Raymond Blanc grew up in Bescanon, a small town in France close to the Swiss border. Despite his parents' plans for him to be an architect, it was the world of restaurants that appealed, and with no formal apprenticeship, Raymond launched himself into the culinary world.

He became a waiter near his home, and in 1972 came to England to become, almost by chance, *chef de rang* at the 'Rose Revived Inn', Newbridge, Oxfordshire; he thus began to establish a reputation as a chef of rare distinction and intuition. He continued his education at the Hotel Wiesbaden, West Germany before returning to Oxford in 1975 to open the first of a succession of restaurants. In 1977, Raymond and his wife Jenny opened *Les Quat' Saisons*, in Summertown, Oxford; in 1979 the restaurant received its first Michelin Star and was proclaimed Egon Ronay Restaurant of the Year. In 1983 it was awarded its second Michelin Star. In 1984 the wealth of experience gained culminated in the opening of *Le Manoir aux Quat' Saisons* at Great Milton.

The Manor House has 15th century origins, with wings added around 1600, and various addi-tions made throughout the years. In 1908 the house was virtually doubled in size by a sympathetic ex-tension constructed in brown ironstone. Most of the windows in the front of the house date from this time. The exterior is breathtaking in its Eng-lishness (in contrast to its charming 'Frenchness' inside). The ancient gate, with a shaped gable above it, is right on the road, near the parish church of St Mary. The gate is no longer in use, instead a new drive sweeps up to the front of the house through two sets of gate-piers and tall trees. In the grounds there is a 17th century dovecote, and an enchanting water garden. The extensive lawns, complete with croquet hoops, may perhaps be the most manicured they have ever been, but they add to the elegant atmosphere throughout.

Inside the house the efficient and courteous young staff discretely bustle about to make pa-trons feel welcome and comfortable. The dining room consists of two interconnecting rooms, pre-dominantly pink, with low beamed ceilings. One room is situated in the manor's old hall (the hall was divided by a floor in the 17th century); a delightful bay window looks out on to the terrace and the gardens beyond. Once within the dining room, one discovers its *raison d'etre* , the reason for eating; there is a choice of the Menu Gourmand (£48.00), which changes weekly, or the Menu du Jour (£19.50) which changes daily. There are win-ter specialities such as *Charlotte d'aubergine et poivrons doux* (a paté of aubergines and sweet peppers), and *Tagliatelles aux truffes fraiches* (home-made fresh pasta garnished with fresh grated truffles). Fish is well represented; *Blanc de barbue, braise aux graines de moutarde* (Fillet of Brill, served with a delicate juice, infused with mustard seed sauce), and *Filet de daurade fumé au charbon de bois, son coulis de tomates crues a l'huile d'anchois* (Wood smoked fillet of Royal sea bream, served with fresh tomato coulis scented with anchovy oil). For the

A QUAT' SAISONS BEDROOM

THE DINING ROOM, WITH THE GARDENS BEYOND

LE MANOIR AUX QUAT' SAISONS

meat course there is *Cuisse et Rable de lapin braise au vin de Banyuls* (Leg and saddle of rabbit, braised in 'Banyuls' red wine, garnished with roasted shallots and wild mushrooms) or *Medaillon de Boeuf roti, sauce Perigourdine* (Roasted fillet of Aberdeen Angus/Charolais beef, served with a red wine sauce scented with truffle juice). The menu changes with the seasons, and is supplemented by an expensive, but carefully chosen, wine list .

Le Manoir is also an hotel, with ten handsomely designed and very comfortable bedrooms, with en suite bathrooms, where every attention to detail has been observed, including such touches as a decanter of Maderia and crystal glasses, and a bowl of exotic fruit. Bed and breakfast can cost somewhere between £150 and £300 for two.

For its efforts *Le Manoir aux Quat'Saisons* has been awarded 2 Michelin Stars (Number Two Best Restaurant of Great Britain), 3 Egon Ronay Stars (86%) (Number One Best Restaurant of the Year 1985), 3 Red AA Guide Stars (Number One Restaurant of Great Britain), and was elected 'Best Restaurant of Great Britain' by the Good Food Guide. It is also a member the prestigious 'Relais & Chateaux'.

A visit to *Le Manoir aux Quat'Saisons* is both a treat for the senses, and a strain on the wallet. But the one fully vindicates the other. It will prove to be an unforgettable experience.

THE ENCHANTING WATER GARDENS

THE CROQUET LAWN

....natural but was in fact created in the early 19th century. Many houses fell into disrepair, but are now undergoing renovation. The Falkland Arms, named after the Viscount Falkland who lived in the big house up the hill, is one of the finest pubs in the county, alongside which are tea rooms and a post office that seem to belong on a film set.
Population: 158. Map Ref: D 4.

CHURCH
St Michael
The church is situated down an elegant shrublined path and is mainly 14th century although it was originally Norman. It has some excellent old bench ends.

PUBLIC HOUSE
The Falkland Arms
Tel: (060 883) 653
The Falkland Arms is a traditional country pub unspoilt by time or man. Truly unique.
Free House. Licensee: Mr John Milligan. Opening Hours: 11.30am - 2.30pm 6 - 11pm. Food Available: 12 - 2pm. Garden. Children's area. Recommendations: Good Pub Guide.

🐾 🐾 🐾 🐾 🐾 🐾 🐾

HAILEY
One end of this village is called Delly End, the other is Poffley End. There is a green, which the houses surround, and a lovely Georgian manor.
Population: 158. Map Ref: C 7.

CHURCHES
St John Evangelist

PUBLIC HOUSES
The Bird in Hand
White Oak Green. Tel: (099386) 321
The Lamb & Flag
Tel: (0993) 702849

🐾 🐾 🐾 🐾 🐾 🐾 🐾

HAILEY
Since the reorganisation of the counties, there are now two 'Haileys' in Oxfordshire. This one is a charming rural community set in the beautiful undulating countryside near Wallingford.
Map Ref: I12

PUBLIC HOUSE
King William IV
Recommendations: Good Pub Guide

HAMPTON POYLE
A small peaceful village on the river Cherwell. 'Hampton' is derived from the Old English word for 'homestead',to which a certain Sir Walter de la Puile added his Norman name in 1268. The church was built in the same period .
Population: 154. Map Ref: F 6.

CHURCH
St Mary

PUBLIC HOUSE
The Bell Inn
Hampton Poyle. Tel: (08675) 3926

🐾 🐾 🐾 🐾 🐾 🐾 🐾

HANWELL
Lovely yellow ironstone houses around an immaculate green. The church has some interesting stone carvings and overlooks Hanwell Castle.
Population: 183. Map Ref: E 1.

CHURCH
St Peter

PUBLIC HOUSE
The Moon & Sixpence
Tel: (0295) 730544

🐾 🐾 🐾 🐾 🐾 🐾 🐾

HARWELL
Harwell is a fruit farming area with orchards all around, although it is best known for the 700 acre Atomic Energy Research Establishment. The old part of the village has cob and thatch walls and the church is late Norman with a 14th century chancel.
Population: 2,229. Map Ref: F 12.

CHURCH
St Matthew

RESTAURANT
Kingswell Restaurant
Reading Road. Tel: (0235) 835303

PUBLIC HOUSES
Chequers
Tel: (0235) 835374
The Crispin Inn
Burr Street. Tel: (0235) 835212
The Kicking Donkey
Tel: (0235) 835344

The White Hart
Tel: (0235) 831872

OTHER AMENITIES
CAR HIRE
Tara Saloon Cars & Limousine Hire
2, The Croft. Tel: (0235) 8341522
SPORTS TRAINING
Silverdown Riding School
Reading Road. Tel: (0235) 835377

🐾 🐾 🐾 🐾 🐾 🐾 🐾

HEADINGTON
Now a suburb of Oxford, Headington was once the site of a Saxon Palace. It is the home of such institutions as the Polytechnic and the John Radcliffe hospital. Stone quarried in Headington was used to build many Oxford colleges. Old Headington has charm and an interesting mix of old and new houses. St Andrew's church was built by a Breton knight in the 12th century.
Population: 7,449. Map Ref: G 8.

PLACES OF INTEREST
The Oxfordshire & Bucks Regimental Museum
Tel: (0865) 716060
Collection of medals, uniforms, badges etc. relating to this regiment, now part of the Royal Green Jackets.

CHURCHES
St Andrew

HOTEL
The Mount Pleasant Hotel
76 London Road. OX3 9AJ Tel: (0865) 62749
Converted cottages offering comfortable accomodation.

GUEST HOUSES
Conifer Guest House
116 The Slade. Tel: (0865) 63055
Dial House
25 London Road. Tel: (0865) 69944
Pickwicks Guest House
17 London Road. Tel: (0865) 750487
Red Mullions Guest House
23 London Road. Tel: (0865) 64727

RESTAURANTS
The Café Francais
146 London Road. Tel: (0865) 62587
Hang Chow Chinese Restaurant
148 London Road. Tel: (0865) 60812
Mirabai Restaurant

70 London Road. Tel: (0865) 62255

PUBLIC HOUSES
The Ampleforth Arms
Colinwood Road. Tel: (0865) 62372
The Bell
72 Old High Street. Tel: (0865) 61594
The Black Boy
Old High Street. Tel: (0865) 63234
The Butchers Arms
5 Wilberforce Street. Tel: (0865) 61252
Chequers Inn
Tel: (0865) 62543
The Crown & Thistle
Old Road. Tel: (0865) 62114
The Fairveiw Inn
Glebeland. Tel: (0865) 63448
The Fox
Tel: (0865) 64572
The Masons Arms
Quarry School Place. Tel: (0865) 64579
The Royal Standard
78 London Road. Tel: (0865) 61490
The Shotover Arms
London Road. Tel: (0865) 62754
The Six Bells
Tel: (0865) 61767
The White Hart
St Andrews Road. Tel: (0865) 61737
Licensee: Mr Maurice K Jacobs.
The White Horse
London Road. Tel: (0865) 62447

OTHER AMENITIES
BOAT HIRE
Howard & Son
58, Sandfield Road. Tel: (0865) 61586
CAR HIRE/SELF DRIVE
Fransman's
4, Lime Walk. Tel: (0865) 63979
CARAVAN PARK
J R Buswell
Wick Farm. Tel: (0865) 63348
CINEMA
Moulin Rouge Cinema
New High Street. Tel: (0865) 63666
GARDEN CENTRE
West & Sons
74, Windmill Road. Tel: (0865) 63556
HOSPITALS
Churchill Hospital
Old Road. Tel: (0865) 64841
John Radcliffe Hospital
Headley Way. Tel: (0865) 64711

THE ANGEL ON THE BRIDGE, HENLEY-ON-THAMES

Park Hospital for Children
Old Road. Tel: (0865) 63461
St Luke's Oxford
4, Latimer Road. Tel: (0865) 750220
LEISURE CENTRE
Northway Centre
Maltfield Road. Tel: (0865) 742048
SAUNA
Parlour
Barton House, Barton Road. Tel: (0865) 65968
SPORTS CLUBS
Headington Bowls Club
Oster Road. Tel: (0865) 61340
Oxford United F C Club
London Road. Tel: (0865) 61503
Oxford United Supporters Club
London Road. Tel: (0865) 63063
Viking Sports Club
67, Old High Street. Tel: (0865) 66335
SPORTS TRAINING
Tennis & Squash Coaching Services
80, Lime Walk. Tel: (0865) 750558
WINE BAR
Café Noir
3, Osler Road. Tel: (0865) 741300

HENLEY-ON-THAMES

Situated on one of the most beautiful reaches of the Thames, spanned by a graceful five-arched bridge built in 1786, appropriately decorated with the faces of Father Thames and the goddess Isis. Henley contains more than 300 buildings of architectural or historic interest, many Georgian buildings, and interesting coaching inns, some with bull and bear-baiting yards. The very first Oxford and Cambridge boat race was held here in 1829, and the world-renowned regatta, established ten years later, is staged in this attractive and prosperous town in early July, attracting visitors from all over the world. The Queen opened a strikingly modern Regatta Headquarters in 1986. The church tower dominates the town, especially when viewed from the river. The churchyard is surrounded by almshouses, and the oldest building in Henley, a Chantry house dating from the 14th century.
Population: 10,910. Map Ref: K 13.

PLACES OF INTEREST
Fawley Court
Designed by Sir Christopher Wren with grounds laid-out by 'Capability' Brown, this museum contains memorabilia

of Polish Kings, and Polish Armed Forces artifacts.
Months Open: March - November. Days Open: Weds, Thurs and Sundays. Hours Open: 2-5pm. Bank Holidays: Closed Easter and Whitsun.

Greys Court
Tel: (04917) 529
A Jacobean house with Georgian additions set amid the remains of a 14th century fortified house. The grounds contain a walled garden, an Archbishop's Maze, and an early Tudor donkey wheel well-house.
Months Open: April - September. Days Open: House and Garden: Mon, Wed and Fri.Garden: Monday - Saturday. Hours Open: 2-6pm. Bank Holidays: Closed Good Friday.

CHURCHES
Baptist Chapel
Market Place.
Friends Meeting House
Northfield End.
Holy Trinity
Hardwick Road.
Methodist Chapel
Duke Street.
Sacred Heart (RC)
Vicarage Road.
St Mary
This 13th Century church, has an impressively tall tower in a chequed pattern of flint and stone, topped with pinnacles, built in 1521-47 by the Bishop of Lincoln.
United Reformed Church
Reading Road.

HOTELS
The Anchor
Friday Street. RG9 1AH Tel: (0491) 574753
The Edwardian Hotel
Station Road. RG9 1AT Tel: (0491) 578678
Warm friendly Hotel with personal service.
Flohrs Hotel
15 Northfield End. RG9 2JG Tel: (0491) 573412
Fine Georgian House, cordon bleu restaurant.
BEDROOMS: 4 Single, (3 en suite) B&B £ 29.50 - £ 49.00. 2 Double, (1 en suite) B&B £ 49.00 - £ 69.00. 4 Twin, (2 en suite, B&B £ 49.00 - £ 65.00. 4 Family, (2 en suite) £ 59.00 - £ 75.00. RESTAURANT: Gourmet Cuisine. Lunch: £ 13.00. Tea: £ 1.50. Dinner: £ 13.00. House Wine: £ 6.50. À La Carte: £ 13.00. Specialities: Menu changes every 3 weeks. HOTEL INFORMATION: CF. W. B. F. 6 space Car Park. Dogs. Credit Cards: AC. AM. D. V. Recommendations: AA**.
The Horse & Groom
40 New Street. Tel: (0491) 575719
BEDROOMS: 2 Double, 2 Twin, Credit Cards: AC.
The Little White Hart Hotel
Riverside. RG9 2LJ Tel: (0491) 574145

Hotel facing Thames, walled garden, traditional ales.
Phyllis Court Club
Marlow Road. RG9 2HT Tel: (0491) 574366
Private members club on the banks of the Thames.
BEDROOMS: 1 Single,(1 en suite, 1 TV, 1 phone, 1 tea/coffee) B&B £ 55.00 - £ 80.00. 1 Double, (1 en suite, 1 TV, 1 phone, 1 tea/coffee) 7 Twin, (7 en suite, 7 TV, 7 phone, 7 tea/coffee) RESTAURANT: English/French Cuisine. Lunch: £ 12.00. Tea: £ 3.00. Dinner: £ 15.00. House Wine: £ 5.75. À La Carte: £ 20.00. Available to non-club members on bedroom occupancy only. Credit Cards: AC. AM. D. V. Recommendations: Johansen.
The Red Lion Hotel
Riverside. RG9 2AR Tel: (0491) 572161
The Regency House Hotel
4 River Terrace. RG9 1BG Tel: (0491) 571133
The Rose and Crown Inn
New Street. RG9 1BG Tel: (0491) 578376
15th century Inn, with well furnished bedrooms & cordon bleu cooking.
The Royal Hotel
51 Station Road. RG9 1AT Tel: (0491) 577526
Thamesmead House Hotel
Remenham Lane. RG9 2LR Tel: (0491) 574745

GUEST HOUSE
J D Williams
3 Western Road. Tel: (0491) 573468

RESTAURANTS
The Alpenhutte Restaurant
41 Station Road. RG9 1AT Tel: (0491) 574165
German and Austrian Cuisine. Specialities: Sauerkraut Bavarian-style; Apfelstrudel Paprika Goulash. Hours Open: Lunch: Closed. Tea: Closed. Dinner: 7-11pm. Last Orders: 9pm week days 10pm weekends . House Wine: £ 5.90. Credit Cards: AC. AM. D. V. Seating Capacity: 30. Vegetarian. Wheelchair. Banquets. Parties. Weddings. Recommendations: AA.
The Angel on The Bridge
Thameside. RG9 1BH Tel: (0491) 574977
Antico
51 Market Place. Tel: (0491) 573060
The Argyll
Market Place. Tel: (0491) 573400
Barnabys Restaurant
2 New Street. RG9 2BT Tel: (0491) 572421
The British Raj Restaurant
21 Reading Road. Tel: (0491) 572218
The Brown Trout
53 Reading Road. RG9 1AB Tel: (0491) 574659
The Casa Nostra
59 Reading Road. RG9 1AB Tel: (0491) 573998
The Catherine Wheel
Hart Street. RG9 2AR Tel: (0491) 573100

The Chef Peking
10 Market Place. Tel: (0491) 578681
The Copper Kettle
18 Thames Side. RG9 1BH Tel: (0491) 575262
Crispins Licensed Restaurant
Bridge House
52 Hart Street. RG9 2AU Tel: (0491) 574232
The Eros Restaurant
6 Duke Street. RG9 1UP Tel: (0491) 574650
Flohrs Hotel and Restaurant
Northfield End . Tel: (0491) 573412
The Gazal Restaurant
53 Reading Road. RG9 1AB Tel: (0491) 574659
Indian Cuisine. Hours Open: Lunch: 12-2.30pm. Dinner: 6-
11.30pm. Last Orders: 11.30pm. Seating Capacity: 50.
Gulshan Tandoori
16 Reading Road. Tel: (0491) 578490
Hanks
37 Hart Street. Tel: (0491) 571733
Old Rope Walk
Hart Street. RG9 2AU Tel: (0491) 574595
English Cuisine. Specialities: Homemade steak and kidney pie;
Home made cakes. Lunch: 12-2.15pm. Tea: 2.30-5.30pm. Lunch:
£ 5.00. Tea: £ 2.50. House Wine: £ 5.00. Seating Capacity: 60.
Veg. W/chair. Parties.
The Old White Hart
Hart Street. Tel: (0491) 573103
The Pearl River
22 Hart Street. Tel: (0491) 578869
The Queens Head
30 Duke Street. RG9 1UP Tel: (0491) 572172
The Regatta Cafe
4 Station Approach. Tel: (0491) 574609
The Row Barge
West Street. Tel: (0491) 572649
Stallones
16-18 Hart Street. Tel: (0491) 579392
The Viceroy Tandoori Restaurant
40 Hart Street. RG9 2AU Tel: (0491) 577097
Indian Cuisine. Specialities: Tandoori dishes. Hours Open:
Lunch: 12-2.30pm. Tea: 6pm. Dinner: 11pm-3 am. Last Orders:
11.15pm. Credit Cards: AC. AM. V. Seating Capacity: 100.
Veg. W/chair. Banquets. Parties. Weddings.
The Victoria
Market Place. RG9 2AA Tel: (0491) 575628
Wimpey
6 Duke Street. Tel: (0491) 576347
Ye Olde Bell
Bell Street. RG9 2BG Tel: (0491) 573883

PUBLIC HOUSES

The Argyll
Market Place. Tel: (0491) 573400
The Bird in Hand

61 Greys Road. Tel: (0491) 575775
The Dukes
Duke Street. Tel: (0491) 572471
The Jolly Waterman
Reading Road. Tel: (0491) 573055
The Kings Arms
Market Place. Tel: (0491) 575458
The Sun Inn
Northfield End. Tel: (0491) 573156
The Three Horseshoes
Reading Road. Tel: (0491) 573971
The Three Tuns
Market Place. Tel: (0491) 573260
A 400 year old pub offering all day service for drinks and
sensibly priced foods.
Brewery: Brakspear. Licensees: Mr & Mrs Jack Knowles. Open-
ing Hours: 10 am - 11 pm Mon-Sat. Noon - 10.30 pm Sunday.
Food Available: 10am - 9.30 pm Mon-Sat. Noon - 9pm Sunday.
Garden. Recommendations: Good Pub Guide.
The Victoria
Market Place. Tel: (0491) 575628
The Wheatsheaf
Reading Road. Tel: (0491) 573234

OTHER AMENITIES

ART GALLERIES
Barry M Keene Gallery
12, Thameside. RG9 1BH Tel: (0491) 577119
Bohun Gallery
15, Reading Road. RG9 1AB Tel: (0491) 576228
Century Galleries Ltd
Thameside. Tel: (0491) 575499
Christopher Selkirk Art Gallery
7, Friday Street. Tel: (0491) 574077
BOAT HIRE
Hobbs and Sons Ltd
Station Road. RG9 1AZ Tel: (0491) 572035
Boat hirers and passenger boat operators.
Months Open: Easter to Mid October. Days Open: All week.
Hours Open: 9 am to 6.30 pm. Self drive day launches and
holiday cruiser hire in the most beautiful part of the River
Thames. Passenger boat trips on the famous Henley Reach.
Rates: On application. Proprietor: W A B Hobbs.
Windsor Belle Ltd.
Boston Road. Tel: (0491) 578822
CAR HIRE/SELF DRIVE
Autodrive
94, Bell Street. Tel: (0491) 575868
Farm Facilities Ltd
94, Bell Street. Tel: (0491) 576022
Ford Rent a Car
Talbot Garage, Station Road. RG9 1AY
Tel: (0491) 574646
CARAVAN PARK

A VIEW DOWNSTREAM FROM HENLEY-ON-THAMES

Swiss Farm International Camping
Swiss Farm, Marlow Road. Tel: (0491) 573419
STORES
Facy Limited
25/31, Market Place. Tel: (0491) 576969
McIlroys
29/31, Bell Street. Tel: (0491) 579678
Woolworths plc
9, Bell Street. Tel: (0491) 572005
GARDEN CENTRES
Cook
Wargrave Road. Tel: (0491) 575174
Toad Hall Garden Centre
Marlow Road. Tel: (0491) 574615
HEALTH CLUB
Rudi Kartal Health Club
20, Duke Street. Tel: (0491) 572056
HOSPITALS
Smith Hospital
Fairmile. Tel: (0491) 572678
Townlands Hospital
York Road. Tel: (0491) 572544
LEISURE CENTRE
Henley & District Indoor Sports Centre
Gillotts Lane. Tel: (0491) 577909
RAILWAY STATION
Henley Station
Station Road. Tel: (0491) 574211
SPORTS CLUBS
Henley Boxing & Boys Club
Outdoor Sports Centre, Mill Lane. Tel: (0491) 578886

Henley Hockey Club
The Sports Centre, Mill Lane. Tel: (0491) 576988
Henley RFC
Dry Leas, Marlow Road. Tel: (0491) 574499
Henley Royal Regatta
Regatta Headquarters, Henley Bridge. Tel: (0491) 572153
THEATRE
Kenton Theatre
New Street. Tel: (0491) 575698
TOURS AND SIGHTS
Driver Guides
5, Ravenscroft Road. RG9 2DH Tel: (0491) 572384

🦢 🦢 🦢 🦢 🦢 🦢 🦢

HETHE

A tiny village situated on a high ridge above Bicester, with a manor house and a church with a wooden turret. There is a small Roman Catholic chapel and priest house.
Population: 280. Map Ref: H 4.

CHURCHES
Holy Trinity (RC)
St Edmund & St George

PUBLIC HOUSE

The Whitmore Arms
Tel: (08697) 654

🦢 🦢 🦢 🦢 🦢 🦢 🦢

HIGHMOOR CROSS

Small village north-west of Henley-on-Thames.
Map Ref: J 13.

CHURCH
St Paul
Simple Victorian church.

PUBLIC HOUSES

The Rising Sun
Witheridge Hill. Tel: (0491) 641455

🐾 🐾 🐾 🐾 🐾 🐾 🐾

HOLTON
Population: 372. Map Ref: H 8.

AMENITIES
LEISURE CENTRE
Park Sports Centre
OX9 1QZ Tel: (08677) 2128
Sports/Leisure Centre
Months Open: All year. Days Open: All week. Hours Open: 9 am
- 11 pm (or longer). Open most Bank Holidays. Sports Hall.
Squash Courts. Conditioning Room. Lounge Bar. Snack counter.
Courses, sessions, casual use in large range of activities for all
ages and abilities. Club bookings, special events, children's holi-
day programmes. Open to non-members. Rates: Current charges
available from the centre. Proprietor: Jeff Hart.

🐾 🐾 🐾 🐾 🐾 🐾 🐾

HOOK NORTON
Hook Norton has been the home of the brewery of
the same name, since 1849. Industries in the past
have included ironworking, weaving and pottery.
The ironstone village is attractive and from the
centre there are lanes and steps leading to a little
stream which flows through the southern side and
across the disused railway line. The railway is now
a nature reserve and may be visited.
Population: 1,657. Map Ref: C 3.

CHURCHES
Baptist Chapel
Methodist Chapel
St Peter
Dominates the centre of the village ; 15th century tower
with pennanted pinnacles. It has an impressive interior
with unusual windows and carvings.

PUBLIC HOUSES
The Bell Inn

High Street. Tel: (0608) 737432
The Gate Hangs High
Tel: (0608) 737387
Licensee: Mr S C Rust.
The Red Lion
Tel: (0608) 737720
The Sun Inn
Tel: (0608) 737570

OTHER AMENITIES
MUSEUM
Pottery and Craft Gallery
East End Farmhouse. Tel: (0608) 737414

🐾 🐾 🐾 🐾 🐾 🐾 🐾

HORLEY
A linear ironstone village standing on an escarp-
ment that runs for some miles along the length the
Warwickshire border.
Map Ref: E 1.

CHURCH
St Ethelreda

PUBLIC HOUSE
The Red Lion Inn
Tel: (0295) 730427
15th century, thatched traditional British pub.
Brewery: Courage. Licensee: Mr B Wood. Opening Hours: Mon-
Fri 10.30am - 2.30pm 6 - 11.00pm . Sat 10.30am - 3.00pm 7.00
- 11.00pm. Sun 12 -3pm 7 - 10.30pm. Food Available: 12 -2pm
7 - 10pm. Restaurant specialities, full menu, Sunday lunch.
Garden.

🐾 🐾 🐾 🐾 🐾 🐾 🐾

HORNTON
Horton has been famous for centuries for the building stone, which was extensively quarried all
around; it is a pale greenish colour when cut, but
the iron veins oxidise and penetrate through the
stone, making it turn orange.
Population: 303. Map Ref: D 1.

CHURCHES
Methodist Chapel
St John Baptist

PUBLIC HOUSE
The Dun Cow
West End. Tel: (029587) 524

🐾 🐾 🐾 🐾 🐾 🐾 🐾

HORSPATH

A village east of Oxford which has a wonderful church with heavy arches in the Transitional style between Norman and Early English, and an interesting stained glass window.
Population: 1,618. Map Ref: H 9.

CHURCH
St Giles

PUBLIC HOUSE
Chequers
Tel: (08677) 2401

🌯 🌯 🌯 🌯 🌯 🌯 🌯

HORTON-CUM-STUDLEY
Map Ref: H 7.

HOTEL
Studley Priory Hotel
OX9 1AZ Tel: (086 735) 203
BEDROOMS: 6 Single, (6 en suite, 6 TV, 6 phone, 6 tea/coffee) B&B £ 60.00 - £ 80.00. 6 Double, (6 en suite, 6 TV, 6 phone, 6 tea/coffee,)B&B £ 75.00 - £110.00. 6 Twin, (6 en suite, 6 TV, 6 phone, 6 tea/coffee)B&B £ 75.00 - £ 110.00. Four Poster. 1 Suite. RESTAURANT: English/French Cuisine. Lunch: £ 22.50. Dinner: £ 22.50. House Wine: £ 7.50. À La Carte: £ 30.00. HOTEL INFORMATION: C.W.B.F. 100 space Car Park. Credit Cards: AC. AM. D. V. Recommendations: AA***. ER. M. RAC. **Weekend Breaks: 2 nights: £ 90.00. 3 nights: £ 135.00. Allowance towards dinner: £ 22.50.**

🌯 🌯 🌯 🌯 🌯 🌯 🌯

IFFLEY

A village that has been established for a thousand years. There is a stone next to the old lock that marks the spot where Iffley Mill was situated, a famous beauty spot until it burnt down in 1908.
Map Ref: F 8.

CHURCH
St Mary
Built between 1154 and 1189, an excellent example of a 12th century parish church. The enormous yew tree in the churchyard is extremely old.

HOTELS
The Elms Hotel
Church Way. OX4 4DZ Tel: (0865) 774449
The Tree Hotel
OX4 4EY Tel: (0865) 775974
Victorian hotel in small village. One mile city centre.

STUDLEY PRIORY HOTEL

PUBLIC HOUSES
The Isis Tavern Riverside
Iffley Lock. Tel: (0865) 247006
The Prince of Wales
Churchway. Tel: (0865) 778542
Situated in the heart of Iffley conservation village. Two minutes from the Isis and the lock.
Brewery: Wadworth. Licensee: Mr S T Cordery. Opening Hours: 11 - 2.30pm   6 - 11pm (Sunday 10.30pm). Food Available: 12 - 2.15pm   6 - 9pm. Specialities: Danish open sandwiches, large vegetarian menu, a large selection of hot and cold food. Garden.

🌯 🌯 🌯 🌯 🌯 🌯 🌯

IPSDEN

Near to the prehistoric Ickield Way, Ipsden is spread on a hillside, and enjoys splendid views.
Map Ref: H 12

PLACES OF INTEREST
Well Place Bird Farm
Tel: (0491) 680092
Home of over 70 different types of birds, with other attractions such as monkeys, foxes, goats and badgers.
Open: Easter - Sept, Oct. - Easter. Days Open: Easter - Sept. Daily. October - Easter Sat and Sun. Hours Open: From 10am. Closed during winter if bad weather. Bank Holidays: Open.

CHURCH
St Mary

KELMSCOTT MANOR, FORMERLY THE HOME OF WILLIAM MORRIS

PUBLIC HOUSE
The White House
Tel: (0491) 35159

🐾 🐾 🐾 🐾 🐾 🐾 🐾

ISLIP
Islip is situated near the confluence of the rivers Cherwell and Ray, famed for its eels in the 17th century. Edward the Confessor, the founder of Westminster Abbey, was born here in 1004. A chapel associated with him was destroyed by a cannonade during the Civil War, and the remains demolished in 1780.
Population: 659. Map Ref: G 7.

PLACES OF INTEREST
Battle Site
The bridge over the river Ray was the scene of several skirmishes during the Civil War 1644/45 , as both Royalists and Parliamentarians fought to gain control of it.

CHURCH
St Nicholas

🐾 🐾 🐾 🐾 🐾 🐾 🐾

KELMSCOTT
Small rural village near the Thames, with an old manor house once inhabited by William Morris.
Map Ref: A 9.

PLACES OF INTEREST
Kelmscott Manor
Elizabethan summer home of writer, designer, craftsman, social reformer William Morris. Family portraits, wallpaper and textiles are on show.
Months Open: April - September. Days Open: 1st Wednesday in each month. Hours Open: 1 - 5pm.

CHURCH
St George
A Norman and Early English church.

PUBLIC HOUSE
The Plough Inn
Tel: (0367) 52358

🐾 🐾 🐾 🐾 🐾 🐾 🐾

KENNINGTON
A large suburb south of Oxford.
Map Ref: F 9.

PUBLIC HOUSES
The Scholar Gypsy
Radley Road. Tel: (0865) 735796
Tandem
21 Kennington Road. Tel: (0865) 735386

OTHER AMENITIES
SPORTS CLUB
Kennington Sports Ground
Tel: (0865) 7366747
UNIVERSITIES/COLLEGES
Templeton College
Kennington Road. Tel: (0865) 735422

☙ ☙ ☙ ☙ ☙ ☙ ☙

KIDLINGTON
Now a satellite of Oxford, this sprawling village has ancient origins; it boasts a beautiful old church in the old part, which is flanked by a row of gabled almshouses.
Population: 12,267. Market day: Friday. Early closing: Monday/Wednesday. Map Ref: F 7.

CHURCHES
Baptist Chapel
St John
St Mary
Rebuilt in the 14th century. It is large and airy with a superb display of medieval glass. The spire is 170 ft high and is a prominent landmark across the valley .

HOTELS
The Black Horse
Banbury Road. Tel: (08675) 3154
Bowood House Hotel
238 Oxford Road. OX5 1EB. Tel: (08675) 2839
4 miles from Oxford, Bowood House offers accommodation of a high standard and a warm , friendly atmosphere.
BEDROOMS: 5 Single, (3 en suite, 5 TV, 5 phone, 5 tea/coffee) B&B £ 25.00 - £ 35.00. 8 Double, (8 en suite, 8 TV, 8 phone, 8 tea/coffee)B&B £ 48.00 - £ 48.00. 5 Twin, (3 en suite, 3 TV, 3 phone, 3 tea/coffee)B&B £ 48.00 - £ 48.00. 2 Family, (2 en suite, 2 TV, 2 phone, 2 tea/coffee) RESTAURANT: English Cuisine. Dinner: £ 12.00. Credit Cards: AC. Am. D. V. Recommendations: AA.

GUEST HOUSE
York Guest House
78 Banbury Road. Tel: (08675) 5460

RESTAURANTS
The Koh-i-noor Tandoori
63 High Street. Tel: (08675) 2245

IndianTandoori Cuisine. Credit Cards: Ac. V. Outdoor eating. Vegetarian. Parties.
Ovisher Restaurant
11 Oxford Road. Tel: (08675) 2827
Pak Ho
25/28 Fairfax Centre. Tel: (08675) 79028

PUBLIC HOUSES
The Squire Bassett
Oxford Road. Tel: (08675) 79340
The Wise Alderman
Tel: (08675) 2281

OTHER AMENITIES
BOAT HIRE
Paddlers
117, Mill Street. OX5 2EE Tel: (08675) 3115
Kayak/Canoe Instruction sessions and hire
Months Open: From April. Kayak instruction for small groups around Oxford's backwaters. Fully qualified instruction and all equipment. Complete novices catered for. Guiding and open canoe trips also available. You come to us or we come to you. Proprietor: David Surman.
CAR HIRE
Oxford Executive Limousine Services
28, Wilsdon Way. Tel: (0865) 728448
GOLF CLUB
North Oxford GC
Tel: (0865) 53977
LEISURE CENTRE
Kidlington & Gosford Sports Centre
Gosford Hill. OX5 2NY Tel: (08675) 6368
Months Open: All year. Days Open: All week. Hours Open: 7 am - 11 pm. 10 am - 6 pm Bank Holidays.
TOURS AND SIGHTS
Oxontours
117, Mill Street. OX5 2EE Tel: (08675) 3115

☙ ☙ ☙ ☙ ☙ ☙ ☙

KINGHAM
Set in the woodlands of Wychwood, and near the River Evenlode, this small Cotswold farming village is popular with ornithologists due to the variety of rare birds which abound. It has won the Best Kept Village competition several times, no doubt partly due to the enchanting green, complete with duck pond.
Population: 571. Early closing: Wednesday. Map Ref: B 4.

CHURCH
St Andrew
Mainly 14th century, has had many changes in succeeding centuries; it has some unique Victorian stone pew ends.

HOTELS

Conygree Gate Country House Hotel
Church Street. Tel: (060 871) 389
BEDROOMS: 1 Single, (1 TV, 1 tea/coffee) B&B £ 16.00*
2 Double, (2 TV, 2 tea/coffee) B&B £ 16.00* 2 Twin, (2 TV, 2
tea/coffee) B&B £ 16.00*. 3 Family, (3 TV, 3 tea/coffee)
£ 16.00* House Wine: £ 6.50. Sports Facilities: Golf nearby.
Riding nearby. Recommendations: AA**. *per person
The Mill House Hotel/Restaurant
OX7 6UH Tel: (060 871) 8188

OTHER AMENITIES

CARAVAN PARK
Churchill Heath Caravan Site
Tel: (0608) 317
YOUTH HOSTEL
Adlestrop Park
Tel: (0608) 359

🐝 🐝 🐝 🐝 🐝 🐝 🐝

KINGS SUTTON

Map Ref: F 3.

PUBLIC HOUSES

The Bell Inn
The Square. Tel: (0295) 811230
The Three Tuns
Tel: (0295) 811356
The White Horse Inn
Tel: (0295) 811292

OTHER AMENITIES

GARDEN CENTRE
Kings Sutton Nurseries
Mill Lane. Tel: (0295) 812023

🐝 🐝 🐝 🐝 🐝 🐝 🐝

KINGSTON BAGPUIZE

The delightful name is derived from the Norman
'Ralf de Bachepuise' who came over with William
the Conqueror. The village in recent years has
become merged with Southmoor.
Population: 1,813. Map Ref: D 10.

PLACES OF INTEREST

Kingston House
Tel: (0865) 820259
A superb Charles II manor house, with interesting stair-
case, fine paintings and furniture in oak-panelled rooms.
A large mature garden.
Months Open: May, June, September. Days Open: Sunday and
Wednesday. Hours Open: 2.30 - 5.30pm. Bank Holidays: Open

Monday in May and August 2.30 - 5.30pm.

CHURCH
St John Baptist

HOTELS

Fallowfields
Tel: (0865) 820416
The Hind's Head
Witney Road. Tel: (0865) 820204

🐝 🐝 🐝 🐝 🐝 🐝 🐝

KINGSTON BLOUNT

A large village nestling beneath the Ridgeway.
Map Ref: K 10.

CHURCH
St John
A small red brick Victorian church built in 1877.

🐝 🐝 🐝 🐝 🐝 🐝 🐝

KINGSTON LISLE

A small village beneath the Berkshire Downs west
of Wantage. It had royal connections through Henry
II, who passed it on to the Lisle family.
Population: 256. Map Ref: B 11.

PLACES OF INTEREST

Blowing Stone
Site of the famous Blowing Stone, a large perforated sarsen
stone which produces a fog-horn sound. Associated with
King Alfred; it is claimed that the noise made by blowing
into the stone emits a bellowing noise which raised the
troops and warned the neighbourhood in times of danger.
Months Open: All Year. Days Open: Daily. Hours Open:
Dawn-Dusk. Bank Holidays: Open.
Kingston Lisle Park
Tel: (036782) 223
An early 19th century house with a dramatic flying stair-
case and attractive gardens. 14th century church nearby
was formerly the chapel of Lisle.
Months Open: Easter - September. Days Open: Thursday.
Hours Open: 2-5pm. Bank Holidays: Open 2-5pm.

CHURCH
St John Baptist
Interesting murals depicting scenes from John the Baptist.

🐝 🐝 🐝 🐝 🐝 🐝 🐝

OPPOSITE: THE ROMANTIC SETTING OF
KINGSTON LISLE PARK

KINGWOOD COMMON

A tiny hamlet north-west of Henley-on-Thames.
Map Ref: J13.

RESTAURANT

The Grouse and Claret
Stoke Row Road. Tel: (049 17) 359

🐈 🐈 🐈 🐈 🐈 🐈 🐈

KIRTLINGTON

Situated on the east side of the Cherwell valley, Kirtlington was an important centre in Anglo-Saxon times; a great assembly was held there in 977, attended by King Edward the Martyr. There is an impressive 18th century Palladian mansion built by Sir James Dashwood, with 700 acres of grounds laid out by 'Capability' Brown.   The Dashwood family have long been associated with the town, hence the Dashwood Arms.
Population: 824. Map Ref: F 11.

CHURCH

St Mary
Situated in the centre of the village, the church was restored in the Victorian era, but a Norman arch supports the tower, which was completely reconstructed in 1853.

HOTEL

The Dashwood Arms
OX5 3HJ Tel: (0869) 50225

OTHER AMENITIES

SPORTS CLUB
Kirtlington Park Polo Club
Tel: (0869) 50521

🐈 🐈 🐈 🐈 🐈 🐈 🐈

LAMBOURN

The springy turf of Lambourn Down is the scene of strings of highly trained race horses exercising against the backdrop of the Berkshire Downs. The village is in a pleasant downland position, and near the medieval church there are almshouses and an ancient village cross.
Map Ref: B 13.

CHURCH

St Michael

RESTAURANT

Restaurant Paddyfield
29 High Street. Tel: (0488) 71656

Peking & Sze-Chuan Cuisine. Hours Open: Lunch: 12.00 - 2.30. Dinner: 6.00 - 11.30. Credit Cards: Ac. Am. D. V. Seating Capacity: 70. Veg. Banquets. Parties. Weddings.

PUBLIC HOUSES

The Hare & Hounds
Baydon Road. Tel: (0488) 71386
The Lamb Inn
Newbury Street. Tel: (0488) 71552
The Wheelwright Arms
Broadway. Tel: (0488) 71643

OTHER AMENITY

CAR HIRE
G Pottinger
24, Northfields Street. Tel: (0488) 72158

🐈 🐈 🐈 🐈 🐈 🐈 🐈

LANGFORD

Situated in the flat expanse of West Oxfordshire, close to the Gloucestershire border. This parish was mentioned in the Domesday Book among the Royal estates.
Map Ref: A9.

CHURCH

St Matthew
The most important Saxon church in the county. The large central tower can be seen for miles around.

PUBLIC HOUSE

The Crown Inn
Tel: (036 786) 206

🐈 🐈 🐈 🐈 🐈 🐈 🐈

LAUNTON

A suburb of Bicester. Near the manor farm is an old church with an 800 year old tower.
Population: 1,291. Map Ref: H 5.

CHURCH

St Mary

PUBLIC HOUSE

The Bull Inn
Bicester Road. Tel: (0869) 253553

🐈 🐈 🐈 🐈 🐈 🐈 🐈

LETCOMBE BASSETT

Letcombe Bassett is one of the highest villages on

the Berkshire Downs, and has a brook , with watercress beds, running through its centre. There are thatched houses surrounding the simple church. The village is actually named after a Norman lord.
Population: 185. Map Ref: C 12.

CHURCH
St Michael

PUBLIC HOUSE
The Yew Tree Inn
Tel: (02357) 3140

𝕒 𝕒 𝕒 𝕒 𝕒 𝕒 𝕒

LETCOMBE REGIS
A large village with modern houses and old cottages and a mixed period church.
Population: 505. Map Ref: D 12.

PLACES OF INTEREST
The Ridgeway Centre
Britain's oldest footpath, it has linked Dorset to the Wash in East Anglia since prehistoric times. This centre is for walkers, horse riders, and cyclists and there is a display room showing exhibits related to the Ridgeway.

CHURCH
St Andrew

HOTEL
The Greyhound
OX12 9JL Tel: (02357) 3023

PUBLIC HOUSE
The Sparrow Inn
Tel: (02357) 3228
Recommendations: Good Pub Guide.

𝕒 𝕒 𝕒 𝕒 𝕒 𝕒 𝕒

LEW
Map Ref: C 8.

CHURCH
Holy Trinity

RESTAURANT
The Farmhouse Hotel
Tel: (0993) 850297
English Homemade Country Cooking . Specialities: Roast meats. Hours Open: Dinner: 7pm. Last Orders: 9pm. Dinner: £ 13.50. House Wine: £ 7.50. Seating Capacity: 80. N/S Areas. Veg. W/ chair. Parties. Weddings. Recommendations: AA.M.

LEWKNOR
A surprisingly quiet village near the M40, tucked into the base of the hills, comprising brick houses and cottages. There is an elegant Georgian former vicarage, and Church Farm, which has a medieval barn. There is a small nature reserve nearby called Lewknor Copse.
Population: 651. Map Ref: J 10.

CHURCH
St Margaret
A mostly Norman church.The clock in the tower has a huge pendulum sunk into the floor.

PUBLIC HOUSE
The Leather Bottle
Tel: (0844) 51482

𝕒 𝕒 𝕒 𝕒 𝕒 𝕒 𝕒

LITTLE COXWELL
A small village close to Great Coxwell with stone cottages and a small church.
Map Ref: B 3.

PUBLIC HOUSE
The Plough Inn
Tel: (0367) 20583

𝕒 𝕒 𝕒 𝕒 𝕒 𝕒 𝕒

LITTLE MILTON
An attractive village with stone-built thatched cottages and two attractive lodges to the manor.
Map Ref: H 9.

CHURCHES
St James

PUBLIC HOUSES
The Lamb Inn
Tel: (0844) 279527
Recommendations: Good Pub Guide.
The Plough
Tel: (0844) 278180

𝕒 𝕒 𝕒 𝕒 𝕒 𝕒 𝕒

LITTLE ROLLRIGHT
See Great Rollright
Map Ref: C 3.

CHURCH
St Philip

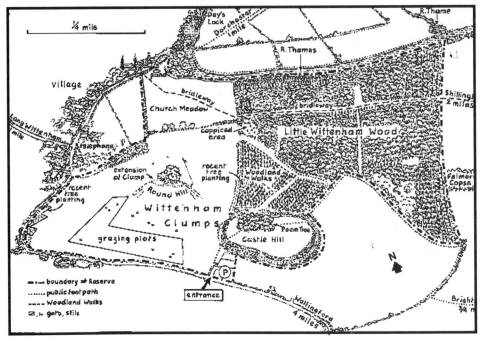

LITTLE WITTENHAM NATURE RESERVE

LITTLE TEW

Down the hill from Great Tew, this is a small pretty village with a Victorian church and lovely old manor house.
Population: 164. Map Ref: D 4.

CHURCHES
Methodist Chapel
St John Evangelist

OTHER AMENITIES
THEATRE
Grange Theatre
The Grange. Tel: (060883) 225

🐾 🐾 🐾 🐾 🐾 🐾 🐾

LITTLE WITTENHAM

Lying beneath the Wittenham Clumps, this village consists of a few houses and cottages which lead down to the church. There is a footpath leading to the smallest lock on the Thames called Day's Lock (see map above).
Population: 68. Map Ref: G 11.

CHURCH
St Peter

OTHER AMENITIES
WILDLIFE PARK
Little Wittenham Nature Reserve
The Manor House. Tel: (086730) 7792
120 acres of land open to the public for informal recreation and woodland walks. Prominent viewpoint on Wittenham Clumps, Iron Age Hillfort and the river Thames.
Months Open: Open Access. Proprietor: Robin Buxton.

🐾 🐾 🐾 🐾 🐾 🐾 🐾

LITTLEMORE

A suburb of Oxford specifically noted for its link with the 19th century churchman John Henry Newman, who was originally a Vicar and shocked the nation by being received into the Roman Catholic church. The group of buildings he lived in are owned by the Oratory Fathers, and there is an exhibition, including Newman's bedroom.
Population: 7,727. Map Ref: G 9.

CHURCHES
St Dominic Barberi (RC)
St Mary & St Nicholas

PUBLIC HOUSES
The George Inn

Tel: (0865) 779341
The Golden Ball
College Lane. Tel: (0865) 779370
The Queens Arms
18 Cowley Road. Tel: (0865) 775511

OTHER AMENITIES
BOAT HIRE
M C L Marina
Heyford Hill Boat Yard. Tel: (0865) 61586
HOSPITAL
Littlemore Hospital
181, Banbury Road. Tel: (0865) 54383
LEISURE CENTRE
Peers Sports & Arts Centre
Sandy Lane West. Tel: (0865) 779348
SPORTS CLUB
Littlemore Rugby Football Club
Peers School. Tel: (0865) 715776

🐦 🐦 🐦 🐦 🐦 🐦 🐦

LITTLEWORTH
A tiny hamlet north-west of Faringdon, in the western part of the county.
Map Ref: B 10.

CHURCH
The Ascension

PUBLIC HOUSE
The Cricketers Arms
Tel: (08677) 2738

🐦 🐦 🐦 🐦 🐦 🐦 🐦

LONG HANBOROUGH
Stretching for two miles, with an old manor house.
Map Ref: D 7.

PLACES OF INTEREST
Oxford Bus Museum
Station Goods Yard.
Tel: (Sec.) (08677) 4080
An interesting growing collection of vehicles from 1915 to 1960. Includes buses from Lisbon and Hong Kong.
Days Open: Weekends.

CHURCH
Christ Church

GUEST HOUSE
Wynford House
79 Main Road. Tel: (0993) 881402

RESTAURANT
The George & Dragon
Tel: (0993) 881362

PUBLIC HOUSE
The Three Horseshoes
Tel: (0993) 881990

OTHER AMENITIES
BOAT HIRE
Oxford Canal Trips
Flagstones, Park Lane. Tel: (0993) 881339

🐦 🐦 🐦 🐦 🐦 🐦 🐦

LONG WITTENHAM
A mile long, this timber and plaster village has a medieval Church Farm and an interesting church.
Population: 890. Map Ref: G 11.

PLACES OF INTEREST
Pendon Museum
Tel: (086730) 7365
Features a historically accurate miniature landscape of the 1930s in exquisite detail.There is also the Madder Valley model railway, created by John Ahern, who pioneered the concept of model railways in a scenic setting.
Months Open: All Year. Days Open: Saturday and Sunday. Hours Open: 11-5pm. Bank Holidays: B H Weekends 11-5pm.
Wittenham Clumps
A tree-crowned chalk knoll marking the site of an ancient hill fort, provides spectacular views, westwards to the Vale of the White Horse, eastwards to the Chiltern Hills.

CHURCH
St Mary
St Mary's has a Norman chancel arch, and an 800 year old font with a design of flowers, wheels and bishops. A figure of a knight in the base of the piscina is 700 years old, the smallest sculptured monument in England.

PUBLIC HOUSES
The Plough Inn
High Street. Tel: (086730) 7738
The Vine Inn
Tel: (086730) 7832

🐦 🐦 🐦 🐦 🐦 🐦 🐦

LONGWORTH
A village centred around the old Rectory, a mainly Georgian house. Barcote Manor, nearby, is a gabled brick mansion built in 1875 in the Tudor style.
Population: 677. Map Ref: D 9.

BASILDON PARK

CHURCH
St Mary
A Perpendicular church with a Jacobean screen. There is a lovely view from the churchyard over the Thames Valley.

PUBLIC HOUSES
The Lamb & Flag
Faringdon Road. Tel: (0865) 820208
The Waggon & Horses Inn
Southmoor. Tel: (0865) 820230

🐾 🐾 🐾 🐾 🐾 🐾 🐾

LOWER ASSENDON
Map Ref: K 13.

PUBLIC HOUSE
The Golden Ball
Tel: (0491) 574157

🐾 🐾 🐾 🐾 🐾 🐾 🐾

LOWER BASILDON
Situated right in the Thames valley between Pangbourne and Streatley.
Map Ref: H 14.

PLACES OF INTEREST
Basildon Park
National Trust. Tel: (07357) 3040
Set in undulating parkland, Basildon Park is an 18th cen-

tury building of Bath stone built by John Carr of York, overlooking the Thames Valley. The focal point of the house is the unusual Octagon room. It contains some interesting plasterwork, fine paintings and furniture.
Months Open: April - October. Days Open: Wednesday and Weekends. Hours Open: Wednesday and Saturday 2-6pm Sunday 12-6pm . Bank Holidays: Bank Holiday Monday 12-6 pm. Closed Good Friday and Wed after B H Mon.
Child Beale Wildlife Trust
Tel: (0491) 671325
A collection of exotic birds and animals set beside the Thames, with riverside walks and a children's play area.
Months Open: Easter-Sept. Open Daily. Hours Open: 10-6pm.

CHURCH
St Bartholomew

RESTAURANT
The Cottage Tearooms and Restaurant
The Cottage, Reading Road. Tel: (0491) 671780

PUBLIC HOUSE
The Crown
Reading Road. Tel: (0491) 671262
Large pub with car park and large garden. Adventure area for children. Pub grub and restaurant. Set in magnificent surroundings.
Brewery: Courage. Licensee: Mr Dennis Miller. Opening Hours: 11 am - 11 pm. Food Available: 11 am - 10 pm. Restaurant Specialities: Chicken stilton, Freedom Aire en crepe. Garden. Children's area.

MAPLEDURHAM HOUSE

LOWER HEYFORD

A small village on the east bank of the Oxford Canal in the Cherwell valley. The village street winds past a group of houses, round the pub and down past the 14th century church. There is an old manor and farm near the canal, and opposite the church is an impressive rectory.

Population: 2,355. Map Ref: F 5.

CHURCH
St Mary

OTHER AMENITIES
BOAT HIRE
Oxfordshire Narrow Boats Ltd
Canal Wharf, Station Road. Tel: (0869) 40348

🐝 🐝 🐝 🐝 🐝 🐝 🐝

LOWER SHIPLAKE

Edwardian riverside village that grew around the railway station on the line to Henley.

Map Ref: K 14.

🐝 🐝 🐝 🐝 🐝 🐝 🐝

MAIDENSGROVE

Map Ref: J12

PUBLIC HOUSE
The Five Horseshoes
Tel: (0491) 641282

MAPLEDURHAM

Surrounded by wooded hills, this village has changed so little that it was chosen as a setting for the 1940s war film, 'The Eagle Has Landed'. There are pretty cottages, 17th century almshouses and an old watermill, the last on the Thames to preserve the wooden machinery. John Galsworthy chose the village as the setting for Soames Forsyte's country house in the 'Forsyte Saga'. Mapledurham House is a fine Elizabethan manor house built in 1588 by Sir Michael Blount, now belonging to the Eyston family. It is open to the public in the summer , when the watermill is also open. At the back of the house there is a little flint parish church which has an aisle owned by the squire partitioned off from the rest of the building. Lord Augustus Fitzclarence, a Victorian rector, disputed the arrangement but lost the case. There is a very pleasant boat-trip to here, up the Thames from Reading.

Population: 313. Map Ref: I 14

PLACES OF INTEREST
Mapledurham House and Water Mill
Tel: (0734) 723350
One of the largest Elizabethan houses in the country standing beside the Thames on the Oxford/Berkshire border. It contains some fine paintings, moulded plasterwork and a beautiful family chapel. There is a riverside picnic park at the restored water-mill that has original machinery and mill stones. The house is said to have inspired Kenneth Grahame's 'Toad Hall'.(See Pangbourne)

ST MARGARET'S CHURCH, MAPLEDURHAM

Months Open: House: Easter - September. Mill: Easter - October, Nov - Easter. Days Open: House: Saturday and Sunday. Mill: Saturday/Sunday (Nov-Easter Sunday). Hours Open: House: 2.30-5pm. Mill: 1.30-5pm (Nov-Easter 2-6pm). Bank Holidays: House : B H Monday 2.30-5pm Mill: 2-6pm.

CHURCH
St Margaret
A mainly 14th and 15th century church, restored in 1863 by William Butterfield, who raised and refaced the tower in a chequered pattern, and added a pyramid roof.

OTHER AMENITIES
BOAT HIRE
D&T Scenics Ltd
RG4 7TR Tel: (0734) 724123
Thames River Cruise (Passenger Boat Operators)
Hours Open: Easter to end September for trips, all year for parties. Rates: On application. Proprietor: T Deaton.

MARCHAM
A village that used to belong to the Abbey of Abingdon. A Georgian house, Denham College,once the home of the Duffield family, is now owned by the National Federation of Women's Institutes, who run residential courses there.
Population: 1,655. Map Ref: E 10.

CHURCH
All Saints

OTHER AMENITIES
GARDEN CENTRE
Hyde Farm Nurseries & Garden Centre
Abingdon Road. Tel: (0865) 391247

MARSTON
A village that was once the focus of the nation's history, when the manor house became the head-quarters of the Parliamentary army.
Population: 3,452. Map Ref: G 8.

CHURCH
St Nicholas
This church was altered in the 15th century, but some parts still remain Norman.

PUBLIC HOUSES
The Friar
Marston Road. Tel: (0865) 244301
The White Hart
Tel: (0865) 23496

MEDMENHAM
Map Ref: K 13.

RESTAURANT
Ye Olde Dog & Badger
Tel: (0491) 571362

MERTON
A pretty village overlooking the river Ray. In AD871 the battle of Mertune between the English and the Danes was fought around here.
Population: 454. Map Ref: H 6.

CHURCH
St Swithun
One of the grandest and most ornate in the county, this church is a good example of the Decorated style, almost untouched by Victorian restoration.

PUBLIC HOUSE
The Plough Inn
Tel: (086 733) 320

MIDDLE ASSENDON
Map Ref: K 12.

PUBLIC HOUSE
The Rainbow Inn
Tel: (0491) 574879
Licensee: R J M Larder.

ʔ ʔ ʔ ʔ ʔ ʔ ʔ

MIDDLE BARTON
A little village through which the Dorn river flows, with old stone houses on either side of a ford.
Map Ref: E 4.

PUBLIC HOUSE
The Carpenters Arms
Tel: (0869) 40378

ʔ ʔ ʔ ʔ ʔ ʔ ʔ

MIDDLETON CHENEY
Map Ref: G 2.

PUBLIC HOUSES
The Dolphin Inn
Tel: (0295) 710314
The New Inn
Tel: (0295) 710399
Licensee: Mr H Ferguson.
The Red Lion Inn
Tel: (0295) 710978

OTHER AMENITIES
CAR HIRE
Cheney Hire Cars Ltd
28, Dands Drive. Tel: (0295) 710965
GARDEN CENTRE
Middleton Home & Garden Centre
Chacombe Road. OX17 2QA Tel: (0295) 710804

ʔ ʔ ʔ ʔ ʔ ʔ ʔ

MIDDLETON STONEY
Consists mainly of a few houses and an inn round a crossroads. The old village was demolished in the 18th century when the Earl of Jersey enlarged his park; only the church remains.
Population: 659. Early closing: Saturday. Map Ref: G 5.

CHURCH
All Saints
Built by the ruins of a Norman castle, All Saints has an interesting 14th century font, which was originally at Islip, and used to be a feeding bowl for turkeys.

HOTEL
The Jersey Arms Inn
Ardley Road. OX6 8SE Tel: (086 989) 234
A Cotswold stone hotel with comfortable rooms.

RESTAURANT
The Rigoletto
Bicester Road. Tel: (086 989) 216

ʔ ʔ ʔ ʔ ʔ ʔ ʔ

MILCOMBE
A small farming village with a few houses, a church and an inn. Milcombe Hall was almost entirely demolished in 1953; all that remains is a pair of 17th century gatepiers and part of the stables. Nearby there is a large and elegant 18th century octagonal dovecote.
Population: 609. Map Ref: E 3.

CHURCH
St Lawrence
Originally built in the 13th century, by the 19th century this church was so dilapidated that it warranted a restoration by G E Street.

HOTEL
The Horse & Groom
Tel: (0295) 720471

ʔ ʔ ʔ ʔ ʔ ʔ ʔ

MILTON
Although near Didcot's power station, and a busy industrial estate, Milton retains its charm with old houses lining the attractive main street.
Map Ref: F 3.

PLACES OF INTEREST
Milton Manor
Tel: (0235) 831287
A delightful 17th century house with Georgian wings, designed by Inigo Jones and set in 20 acres of garden beside a lake. The manor has had many famous visitors, including William of Orange and Peter the Great.
Months Open: Easter-October. Days Open: Weekends. Hours Open: 2-5.30. Bank Holidays: B H Monday 2-5.30.

CHURCH
St Mary

ʔ

MINSTER LOVELL HALL

MILTON COMMON

Map Ref: I 9.

HOTEL
The Belfry Hotel
Brimpton Grange. OX9 2JW Tel: (0844) 279381
Large half-timbered Country House in extensive grounds.

PUBLIC HOUSE
The Three Pigeons
OX9 2NS Tel: (08446) 247

MILTON-UNDER-WYCHWOOD

G E Street is again in evidence in this village, in the church, the school and the school house, all of which he designed.
Population: 1,837. Map Ref: B 6.

CHURCH
St Simon & St Jude
G E Street designed this church in Gothic style.

HOTEL
Hillborough House
The Green. OX7 6JH Tel: (0993) 830501
Victorian Country House Hotel facing the village green, with a cosy bar, conservatory coffee lounge and candlelit Dining Room.

BEDROOMS: 3 Double, (3 en suite, 3 TV, 3 tea/coffee) B&B £ 28.00 - £ 38.00. 2 Twin, (2 en suite, 2 TV, 2 tea/coffee) B&B £ 28.00 - £ 38.00. 1 Family, (1 en suite, 1 TV, 1 tea/coffee) RESTAURANT: English Cuisine. Credit Cards: AC. AM. D. V. Recommendations: AA.
Weekend Breaks: 2 nights: £ 50.00. 3 nights: £ 75.00. Allowance towards dinner: £ 10.00.

MINSTER LOVELL

Situated in a pretty part of the Windrush Valley, Minster Lovell is a village in two parts; the old part is typically Cotswold stone and slated roof. There is an almost untouched 15th century church, and the impressive ruined Hall (see left) was one of the great aristocratic houses in the county, set amongst the trees alongside the river; this and the restored dovecote by the riverside are both maintained by English Heritage. Across the B4047 is the new part of Minster Lovell, with new residences and some light industry. It was here that the Chartists established a community, with each family having enough land to provide for themselves. These were known as the Chartreville Allotments.
Population: 1,344. Map Ref: C 7.

PLACES OF INTEREST
Minster Lovell Hall
Tel: (0993) 75315
A skeleton of Lord Francis Lovell was found in an underground vault after he'd been in hiding from the King, following the Lambert Simnell Rising of 1487. His servant, the only person to know of his whereabouts, unfortunately died, leaving the luckless Lord incarcerated until his skeleton was found in 1718.
Months Open: 15 March - 15 October. Days Open: Daily. Hours Open: Monday - Saturday: 9.30 - 6.30 Sunday: 2 - 6.30.

CHURCH
St Kenelm
Rebuilt in the 15th century; contains an alabaster tomb-chest of one of the Lovells.

HOTELS
The Old Swan Hotel
Main Street. OX8 5RN Tel: (0993) 775614
Charming comfortable Cotswold stone hotel.
BEDROOMS: 2 Single, (2 en suite, 2 TV, 2 phone, 2 tea/coffee) B&B £ 37.50 - £ 42.50. 3 Double, (3 en suite, 3 TV, 3 phone, 3 tea/coffee) B&B £ 54.00 - £ 64.00. 4 Twin, (4 en suite, 4 TV, 4 phone, 4 tea/coffee) 1 Family, (1 en suite, 1 TV, 1 phone, 1 tea/ coffee) 1 Four Poster, £ 64.00. 1 Suite. RESTAURANT: English/French Cuisine. Lunch: £ 10.00. Tea: £ 0.80. Dinner:

£17.50. House Wine: £ 6.95. À La Carte: £ 17.50. Specialities: Local dishes. HOTEL INFORMATION: CF. W. Credit Cards: AC. AM. D. V. Recommendations: AA **. ER. M.

The White Hart
Church Green. OX8 6AZ Tel: (0993) 775255
Overlooking the Church.

PUBLIC HOUSE
The New Inn
Tel: (0993) 775467

🐚 🐚 🐚 🐚 🐚 🐚 🐚

MOLLINGTON
Situated on a hill above the Mollington brook, this attractive ironstone village won an award for the Best-Kept village in the county. The church was built in the 14th century, and looks down on to a Tudor manor and barn.
Population: 460. Map Ref: F 1.

CHURCH
All Saints

PUBLIC HOUSE
The Green Man
Tel: (0295) 750692

🐚 🐚 🐚 🐚 🐚 🐚 🐚

MOULSFORD-ON-THAMES
A Thames-side village nestling beneath the Downs which stretch up behind the village to the west. From the garden of the riverside pub, Brunel's bridge can be seen carrying the railway across the river and over the low-lying land.
Population: 469. Map Ref: H 13.

CHURCH
St John Baptist
The church stands idyllically on the river, and was almost completely rebuilt about 100 years ago.

HOTEL
The Beetle and Wedge Hotel
Ferry Lane. OX10 9JF Tel: (0491) 651376

🐚 🐚 🐚 🐚 🐚 🐚 🐚

NETTLEBED
An old brick kiln is all that remains of a large brick-making industry that gave employment to Nettlebed's inhabitants for over 500 years. In 1365, for example, it was recorded that 35,000 bricks

were supplied for the construction of Wallingford castle. An attractive main street has Georgian houses and creeper-covered inns all built in the local brick. Joyce Grove, a Jacobethan mansion of 1908, is now a Sue Ryder home.
Population: 662. Map Ref: J 12.

CHURCH
St Bartholomew
The 19th century grey and red brick church has two windows stained by John Piper.

HOTELS
The Bull Hotel
19 High Street. Tel: (0491) 641233
The White Hart Hotel
High Street. Tel: (0491) 641245

PUBLIC HOUSES
The Carpenters Arms
Crocker End. Tel: (0491) 641477
Recommendations: Good Pub Guide.
The Sun Inn
4 Watlington Street. Tel: (0491) 641359

OTHER AMENITIES
CAR HIRE
S.Hope
9, Watlington Street. Tel: (0491) 641238
TOURS AND SIGHTS
Country Ways
Merrafield, Crocker End. Tel: (0491) 641364

🐚 🐚 🐚 🐚 🐚 🐚 🐚

NEW YATT
Map Ref: D 7.

PUBLIC HOUSE
The Saddlers Arms
Tel: (099386) 368

A VIEW FROM THE BEETLE AND WEDGE,
MOULSFORD-ON-THAMES

NEWBRIDGE

Map Ref: D 9.

HOTEL
The Rose Revived Inn
OX8 7QD Tel: (086 731) 221

PUBLIC HOUSE
The Maybush Inn
Tel: (086 731) 624
Recommendations: Good Pub Guide.

🐾 🐾 🐾 🐾 🐾 🐾 🐾

NORTH HINKSEY

A village that has gradually become absorbed by Oxford. The area around the church manages to retain a village atmosphere. It was here that Saxons first forded the river to found Oxford.
Population: 4,002. Map Ref: E 8.

PUBLIC HOUSES
Fishes Inn
Tel: (0865) 249796

🐾 🐾 🐾 🐾 🐾 🐾 🐾

NORTH LEIGH

A large village situated on a windmill-topped hill overlooking the Evenlode valley; reminders of pre-Roman times are to be seen in the great earthworks of Grimms Dyke nearby.
Population: 1,851. Map Ref: D 7.

PLACES OF INTEREST
North Leigh Roman Villa
Tel: (0993) 881830
Near Akeman Street, this once splendid Roman 'country house' had an excellent courtyard, 60 rooms, mosaic floors, and underfloor heating.
Months Open: April - September. Days Open: Daily. Hours Open: 9.30am - 6.30pm.

NORTH LEIGH ,MOSAIC FLOOR AT THE ROMAN VILLA

CHURCH
St Mary
Has a Saxon Tower dating from the 11th century. G E Street restored the church in the 19th century adding a stone screen and a new pulpit.

PUBLIC HOUSES
The Leather Bottle
East End. Tel: (0993) 882174
The Woodman
New Yatt Road, Nr Witney. Tel: (0993) 881790

OTHER AMENITIES
GARDEN CENTRE
North Leigh Garden Centre
Tel: (0993) 881372

🐾 🐾 🐾 🐾 🐾 🐾 🐾

NORTH MORETON

An attractive village with 17th century timbered buildings mingled in with modern houses.
Population: 318. Map Ref: G 12.

CHURCH
All Saints
An unaltered 13th century nave and chancel and a chapel built by Sir Miles Stapleton in 1299, who was killed at the Battle of Bannockburn. There is some fine medieval glass.

PUBLIC HOUSE
The Bear Inn
High Street. Tel: (0235) 813236

OTHER AMENITIES
NIGHT CLUB
Rio Night Club
Hadden Hiill. Tel: (0235) 811323

🐾 🐾 🐾 🐾 🐾 🐾 🐾

NORTH NEWINGTON

Map Ref: E 2.

GUEST HOUSE
Mill House
Tel: (0295) 730212

PUBLIC HOUSES
The Bakers Arms Country Inn
Main Street. Tel: (0295) 730650
The Roebuck Inn
Tel: (0295) 730444
Licensee: Mr Alistair Bech.

NORTHMOOR

A lovely village with old stone cottages standing by a brook. There is a Rectory Farm, and a 14th century church.

Population: 355. Map Ref: D 9.

CHURCH
St Denis

PUBLIC HOUSE
The Dun Cow
Tel: (086731) 295

OTHER AMENITIES
CARAVAN PARK
Gowrings Leisure
Thameside Park, Bablock Hythe. Tel: (0865) 880161

🐾 🐾 🐾 🐾 🐾 🐾 🐾

NUFFIELD

A small scattered village sited on a hilltop between Henley-on-Thames and Wallingford, whose name William Morris took when he was elevated to the peerage (see below).

Population: 409. Map Ref: I 12.

PLACES OF INTEREST
Nuffield Place
Tel: (0491) 641224
Built in 1914, in 1933 this house became the home of William Morris, Lord Nuffield, creator of Morris Cars. Some rooms remain the same as he & Lady Nuffield knew them.
Months Open: May - Sept. Days Open: Every 2nd and 4th Sunday. Hours Open: 2-5pm.

PUBLIC HOUSE
The Crown Inn
Tel: (0491) 641335

🐾 🐾 🐾 🐾 🐾 🐾 🐾

NUNEHAM COURTENAY

Simon, first Earl Harcourt rebuilt this village in the 1760's to replace the one he destroyed to avoid distasteful viewing from his new Palladian villa. The buildings were identically designed in chequered brick, and included a forge (now a garage) an inn, a curate's house, a post office. The entire peasantry was moved in 'en masse'; this act was said to have inspired Oliver Goldsmith to write 'The Deserted Village' in 1770.
Map Ref: G 10.

PLACES OF INTEREST
Nuneham Park
Tel: (086 783) 551
Described by Horace Walpole as 'the most beautiful place in the world' the architect Stiff Leadbetter created this magnificent Palladian mansion for Lord Harcourt in the late 18th century. Used now as a conference centre, and owned by Oxford University, it is world famous not only for the beautiful surroundings but also for the design, gardens, temples, follies and statues that are found within its grounds, laid out by the ubiquitous 'Capability' Brown. All Saints chapel (see below) designed by Harcourt himself, is in the grounds.

CHURCH
All Saints
Designed by Lord Harcourt, assisted by James 'Athenian' Stuart, who, as his name suggests, was influenced by the architecture of Greece, although this domed temple owes more to Rome than Athens.

RESTAURANT
The Harcourt Arms
Tel: (0865) 881931

🐾 🐾 🐾 🐾 🐾 🐾 🐾

OT MOOR

Map Ref: H 7.

PLACES OF INTEREST
A low lying wilderness that is of great interest to naturalists, covering 6 square miles. This ancient fen was created by the river Ray and its tributaries; until it was drained in the 19th century, it was a marshland, where the main activities were fishing, fowling and peat cutting. Ot Moor is shaped like a dish, and is surrounded by seven villages; Charlton-on-Otmoor, Beckley, Oddington, Noke, Fencott, Murcott, and Horton-cum-Studley.

A VIEW FROM THE WEST TERRACE OF NUNEHAM PARK

MERTON COLLEGE, OXFORD

OXFORD

Magnificent historic University town, one of the most beautiful in Europe, rich in architecture and atmosphere. It has many ancient colleges, some dating from the 13th century; most notable are Christ Church with the impressive Tom Quad, Tom Tower and Cathedral; Magdalen College which has a lovely deer-park and cloisters; New College; Merton College with Mob Quad; Oxford's oldest, Worcester and St. Johns, which have particularly beautiful gardens. Around Radcliffe Square are clustered some of Oxford's most beautiful and distinctive buildings, particularly the domed Radcliffe Camera, built in 1736. There are many museums, including the Ashmolean, the Museum of Modern Art, and the Frank Cooper shop and Museum of Marmalade. Botanic Gardens, riverside walks, and punting on the Cherwell should all be experienced. Oxford also has a splendid modern shopping centre.
Map Ref: F 8.

PLACES OF INTEREST

Alice's Shop

Tel: (0865) 723793

This shop is where the real Alice used to come and buy her sweets. She was later turned into the fictitious 'Alice in Wonderland' by Lewis Carroll. The shop is a gift and souvenir shop specialising in Alice.

Open daily all year. Hours Open: Summer: Mon-Sat 9.30am-5pm , Sun 10am-3pm. Winter: Mon-Sat: 10am-4.30pm.

Ashmolean Museum

Beaumont Street.

Tel: (0865) 27800

Founded by Elias Ashmole, this is Britain's oldest public museum, dating back to 1683. It contains the University's collection of Michelangelo drawings and Pre-Raphaelite and French impressionist works. Among other collections, it also includes British, European, Egyptian archaeology; Islamic and Asian art.

Months Open: All Year. Days Open: Daily except Monday. Hours Open: Tuesday-Saturday: 2-4pm Sunday: 2-4pm . Bank Holidays: Closed Good Friday, Easter 4-6pm: Bank Holiday Monday open 2-5pm.

Balfour Building

60, Banbury Road.

Tel: (0865) 274726

Musical instruments from around the world.

Months Open: All Year. Days Open: Mon - Sat. Hours Open: 1 - 4.30pm. Bank Holidays: Closed Easter and Xmas.

Frank Cooper's Marmalade Shop

84, High Street.

Tel: (0865) 245125

This famous Oxford export has returned to its original home, and a variety of Cooper's goods are on sale.

Museum of Modern Art

30, Pembroke Street.

Tel: (0865) 722733

Features work by leading international artists. There are educational activities, films and seminars which accompany each exhibition.
Months Open: All Year. Days Open: Daily except Mondays. Hours Open: Tuesday-Saturday: 10am-6pm. Sunday: 2-6pm.

Museum of Oxford
St Aldates.
Tel: (0865) 81559
Records the history of Oxford from prehistoric times to the present day. The rooms have been arranged to show how Oxford inhabitants lived during the ages.
Months Open: All Year. Days Open: Tues - Sat. Hours Open: 10am - 5pm.

Museum of the History of Science
Broad Street.
Tel: (0865) 277280
Early scientific instruments, including astrolobes and microscopes, photographic equipment, clocks and watches, surgeon's instruments. Einstein's blackboard, covered in calculations, is on display.
Months Open: All Year. Days Open: Mon - Fri. Hours Open: 10.30am - 1pm, 2.30 - 4pm. Bank Holidays: Closed.

Oxford Canal
A 90 mile inland waterway between Oxford and Coventry built in 1780, with 250 bridges, 42 locks, warehouses and stables for tow horses.

Oxford University Museum
Parks Road.

TOM TOWER, CHIRST CHURCH, OXFORD

Tel: (0865) 272950
Many of these scientific exhibits are second only in importance to those in the Natural History Museum. There are skeletons of dinosaurs, and models of mammals, birds and reptiles. The model of the dodo is said to have inspired Lewis Carroll to include it in 'Alice in Wonderland'.
Months Open: All Year. Days Open: Mon - Sat. Hours Open: 12 - 5pm.

The Oxford Story
Broad Street.
Tel: (0865) 728822
A Guide to the University where visitors are transported back via a medieval student's desk to experience life in Oxford throughout the ages.
Months Open: All Year. Days Open: Daily. Hours Open: April - October : 9am-7pm , November - March: 9am-5.30pm.

The Pitt Rivers Museum
South Parks Road.
Tel: (0865) 270927
One of Britain's finest collections of the ethnology and archaeology of the people of the world. Exhibits include totem poles, shrunken heads and weapons.
Months Open: All Year. Days Open: Mon - Sat. Hours Open: 1 - 4.30pm. Bank Holidays: Closed Easter and Xmas.

The Rotunda Museum of Antique Dolls' Houses
Grove House, Iffley Turn.
Private collection of over forty Dolls' Houses 1700-1900, plus their contents.
Months Open: May - Sept. Days Open: Sunday afternoon.

CHURCHES

All Saints
High Street.

Catholic Chapel
St Clement's Street.

First Church of Christ, Scientist
St Giles. Tel: (0865) 57605

Keythought Bible Message
Pennyfarthing Place. Tel: (0865) 240438

New Road Baptist Church
Bonn Square. Tel: (0865) 247583

North Gate Hall Methodist Church
St Michael's Street.

Oxford Mosque
Bath Street. Tel: (0865) 245547

Oxford Synagogue and Jewish Centre
Richmond Road. Tel: (0865) 514356

Religious Society of Friends,
St Giles. Tel: (0865) 57373

Sant Nirankari Mandal
Marston Road. Tel: (0865) 240229

St Aldate

St Aloysius
Woodstock Road. Tel: (0865) 57978

THE RADCLIFFE CAMERA

St Andrew
Linton Road.
St Barnabas
Cardigan Street.
St Clement
St Columbia's United Reformed Church
Alfred Street.
St Cross
St Cross Road.
St Ebbe
St Ebbe's Street.
St Giles Church
Woodstock Road. Tel: (0865) 514319
St Margaret
St Margaret's Road.
St Mary
St Mary Magdalen
Magdalen Street.
St Mary The Virgin
High Street. Tel: (0865) 243806
St Michael
Ship Street.
St Michael at the North Gate
Cornmarket Street. Tel: (0865) 240940
Oxford's oldest building. It has a Saxon tower dating from the first half of the eleventh century.
St Paul
Walton Street.

St Peter in the East
Queen's Lane.
St Peter-Le-Bailey
St Peter's College.
St Philip & St James
Woodstock Road.
St Thomas
Becket Street.
United Pentecostal Church
Banbury Road. Tel: (0869) 810448
Wesley Memorial Church
Hall Street. Tel: (0865) 243216
Wesley Memorial Methodist Church
New Inn Hall Street.
Wolvercote Church
Tel: (0865) 515640

HOTELS

The Apollo
61 St Aldgates. Tel: (0865) 242138
The Cape of Good Hope
The Plain. OX4 1AF Tel: (0865) 242570
The Cotswold Lodge Hotel
66a Banbury Road . OX2 6JP Tel: (0865) 512121

Old building with modern facilities & friendly atmosphere
BEDROOMS: 18 Single, (18 en suite, 18 TV, 18 phone, 18 tea/coffee) 12 Double, (12 en suite, 12 TV, 12 phone, 12 tea/coffee) 18 Twin, (18 en suite, 18 TV, 18 phone, 18 tea/coffee) 2 Family, (2 en suite, 2 TV, 2 phone, 2 tea/coffee) RESTAURANT: Varied Cuisine. Lunch: £ 12.00. Tea: £ 2.50. Dinner: £ 15.00. House Wine: £ 6.00. À La Carte: £ 20.00. HOTEL INFORMATION: CF. W. B. F. 50 space Car Park. Credit Cards: AC. AM. D. V. Recommendations: AA ***.
Weekend Breaks: 2 nights: £ 88.75. 3 nights: £ 132.75.
Allowance towards dinner: £ 15.00.
Courtfield Private Hotel
367 Iffley Road. Tel: (0865) 242991
The Eastgate Hotel
23 Merton Street. OX1 4BE Tel: (0865) 248244
BEDROOMS: 11 Single, (11 en suite, 11 TV, 11 phone, 11 tea/

coffee) B&B £ 66.45 - £ 74.45. 22 Double, (22 en suite, 22 TV, 22 phone, 22 tea/coffee) B&B £ 88.00 - £ 108.00. 9 Twin, (9 en suite, 9 TV, 9 phone, 9 tea/coffee) B&B £ 88.00 - £ 108.00. 1 Four Poster:£105.00. 1 Suite. RESTAURANT: Best of British Cuisine. Lunch: £ 8.00. Tea: £ 4.00. Dinner: £ 12.50. House Wine: £ 6.50. À La Carte: £ 15.00. Specialities: Daily Specials. HOTEL INFORMATION: CF. W. B. F. 35 space Car Park. Dogs. N/S. Credit Cards: AC. AM. D. V. Recommendations: AA ***.
Weekend Breaks: 2 nights: £ 92.00. 3 nights: £ 138.00. Allowance towards dinner: £ 12.50.

The Grandpont Arms
Edith Road. OX1 Tel: (0865) 241788
The King's Guest House
226 Iffley Road. OX4 1SE Tel: (0865) 248649
Ladbroke Linton Lodge
Linton Road. OX2 6UJ Tel: (0865) 53461
This Hotel has a country house atmosphere, and the oak-panelled restaurant with its fascinating collection of Edwardiana provides a delightful setting for dinner.
BEDROOMS: 17 Single, (17 en suite, 17 TV, 17 phone, 17 tea/coffee) B&B £ 43.00 - £ 60.00*. 18 Double, (18 en suite, 18 TV, 18 phone, 18 tea/coffee) B&B £ 28.00per person- £ 75.00*. 34 Twin, (34 en suite, 34 TV, 34 phone, 34 tea/coffee) B&B £ 28.00pp - £ 75.00*. 2 Family, (2 en suite, 2 TV, 2 phone, 2 tea/coffee) £ 38.00pp - £ 85.00*. 1 Four Poster. RESTAURANT: Carvery Cuisine. Lunch:£ 8.50. Dinner: £ 11.50. House Wine: £ 7.10. HOTEL INFORMATION: CF. W. B. F. 40 space Car Park. Dogs. NS. Credit Cards: AC. AM. D. V. Recommendations: AA. ER. (* Not including breakfast)
Weekend Breaks: 2 nights: £ 38.00. 3 n: £ 28.00.(per night)
The Old Black Horse Hotel
102 St. Clements. OX4 1AR Tel: (0865) 244691
Close to city centre, Magdalen bridge and High Street.
The Old Parsonage Hotel
3 Banbury Road. OX2 6NW Tel: (0865) 310210
The Oxford Moat House
Wolvercote Roundabout. OX2 8AL Tel: (0865) 59933
Modern Hotel well situated for the Cotswolds and Oxford.
BEDROOMS: 4 Double, (3 en suite) B&B £ 30.00 - £ 36.00. 1 Twin, B&B £ 30.00 - £ 36.00. 1 Family, (1 en suite) £ 36.00 - £ 45.00. Recommendations: AA.
Parklands Hotel
100 Banbury Road. OX2 6JU Tel: (0865) 54374
The Pine Castle Hotel
290 Iffley Road. OX4 4AE Tel: (0865) 241497
The Randolph Hotel
Beaumont Street. OX1 2LN Tel: (0865) 247481
Large Victorian hotel with modern facilities.
The River Hotel
17 Botley Road. OX2 0AA Tel: (0865) 243475
Small friendly hotel overlooking Thames.
The Royal Oxford Hotel
Park End Street. Tel: (0865) 248432
The Travelodge Hotel

MERTON TOWER, OXFORD

Peartrees Roundabout. OX2 8JZ Tel: (0865) 54301
The Victoria Hotel
180 Abingdon Road. OX1 4RA Tel: (0865) 724536
Completely modernised Victorian hotel, 10 mins city centre.
Westgate Hotel
1 Botley Road. OX2 0AA Tel: (0865) 726721
Close rail and bus stations, 10 mins walk city centre.
The Westwood Country Hotel
Hinksey Hill Top. OX1 5BG Tel: (0865) 735408
Willow Reaches Hotel
1 Wytham Street. OX1 4SU Tel: (0865) 721545

GUEST HOUSES
Acorn Guest House
260 Iffley Road. Tel: (0865) 247998
Adams Guest House
302 Banbury Road. Tel: (0865) 56118
Anthony's Guest House
255 Cowley Road. Tel: (0865) 243916
The Ascot Guest House
283 Iffley Road. OX4 4AQ. Tel: (0865) 240259/727669
The Athena Guest House
253 Cowley Road. Tel: (0865) 243124
B M Strange
234 Abingdon Road. Tel: (0865) 241767
Becket House
5 Becket Street. Tel: (0865) 724675

THE BOTANIC GARDENS, OXFORD

Bravalla Guest House
242 Iffley Road. Tel: (0865) 241326
Bronte Guest House
282 Iffley Road. Tel: (0865) 244594
The Burren
374 Banbury Road. Tel: (0865) 513513
Casa Villa Guest House
388 Banbury Road. OX2 7PW. Tel: (0865) 512642
This Guest House has comfortable bedrooms, an attractive dining room, and à la carte menu.
Months Open: All year. Number of Bedrooms: 11. (7 with bathroom). B&B per person: £17. TV. Pets. Evening meals. Car park. Garden.
Conbermere House
11 Polstead Road. Tel: (0865) 56971
Earlmont Guest House
322 Cowley Road. Tel: (0865) 240236
Falcon Guest House
90 Abingdon Road. Tel: (0865) 722995
The Green Gables
326 Abingdon Road. Tel: (0865) 725870
Greenviews
95 Sunningwell Road. Tel: (0865) 249603
The Guest House
3 Iffley Road. Tel: (0865) 724629
Hamden Guest House

233 Cowley Road. Tel: (0865) 249578
Highfield West Guest House
188 Cumnor Hill. OX2 9PJ. Tel: (0865) 863007
Highfields Guest House
91 Rose Hill. Tel: (0865) 774083
A pleasing quiet house with good access to the city centre, four large rooms with tea and coffee making facilities.
Months Open: All year. Number of Bedrooms: 4. (2 with bathroom). B&B per person: £12-16. TV. Evening meals. Car Park. Garden.
Isis Guest House
45-53 Iffley Road. OX4 1ED. Tel: (0865) 242466

 37 comfortable rooms with all facilities. Ideally situated for the town centre. Excellent traditional English breakfast and a warm friendly atmosphere.
Months Open: July, August, September. Number of Bedrooms: 37 with TV (14 with bathroom). B&B per person: £15.50 - £17.50. Dogs. 18 space car park. Manager: Mr C. E. Hammond.
Kings Guest House
363 Iffley Road. Tel: (0865) 241363
A friendly run guest house, situated one mile from the centre of Oxford. Delightful garden. RAC and Tourist Board registered.
Open all year. Number of Bedrooms: 5. (3 with bathroom). B&B

THE MOB QUAD, MERTON COLLEGE, OXFORD

per person: £15-20. Evening meals. Car park. Garden.

Lakeside Guest House
118 Abingdon Road. Tel: (0865) 244725
Months Open: All year. Number of Bedrooms: 4. (4 with bathroom). B&B per person: £14. TV. Car park.

Nanford Guest House
137 Iffley Road. Tel: (0865) 244743

Newton House
82-84 Abingdon Road. Tel: (0865) 240561

Norham
16 Norham Road. Tel: (0865) 515352

Northfield House
106 Banbury Road. Tel: (0865) 54222

Old Parsonage Hotel
3 Banbury Road. Tel: (0865) 52229

The Pine Castle Hotel
290 Iffley Road. Tel: (0865) 241497

R C Adams
312 Banbury Road. Tel: (0865) 54872

S Alden
11 Kingston Road. Tel: (0865) 54769

Shiral's Guest House
445 Cowley Road. Tel: (0865) 777195
Very good breakfast. Clean and homely. Good value for money. We also do Car Hire and Minibus.
Number of Bedrooms: 12. (12 with bathroom). B&B per person:

£11 pp. TV. Car park.

Sportsview Guest House
106/108 Abingdon Road. Tel: (0865) 244268

Summertown Guest House
277 Banbury Road. Tel: (0865) 53674

W G B Shannon
329 Cowley Road. Tel: (0865) 247558

The Walton Guest House
169 Walton Street. Tel: (0865) 52137

Whitehouse View
9 Whitehouse Road. Tel: (0865) 721626

Windrush Guest House
11 Iffley Road. Tel: (0865) 247933
Months Open: All year. Number of Bedrooms: 8. TV.

RESTAURANTS

The Akash Tandoori
212 Cowley Road. Tel: (0865) 725217

Baedeckers
43a Cornmarket Street. Tel: (0865) 242063
International Cuisine. Specialities: Peking duck. Lunch: 12. Last Orders: 11.30. Lunch: £8.00. Dinner: £10.00. House Wine: £5.25. Credit Cards: AC. V. Seating Capacity: 100. Veg. Parties.

The Bandung Indonesian & Malaysian
124 Walton Street. Tel: (0865) 511668

NEW COLLEGE, OXFORD

Bevers Wholefood Restaurant
36 St Michaels St. Tel: (0865) 724241
The Blue Coyote
36 St Clement's. Tel: (0865) 241431
Browns Restaurant and Bar
7 Woodstock Road. Tel: (0865) 511995
Byron Restaurant
4 St Ebbes. Tel: (0865) 245078
The Cherwell Boathouse
Bardwell Road. OX2 6SR Tel: (0865) 52746
Credit Cards: AC. AM. D. V. Seating Capacity: 50. Outdoor .
Veg. B. P. W. Recommendations: ER.
The Chit-Chat
1 Broad Street. Tel: (0865) 240973
Italian Cuisine. Specialities: Pastas, Pizzas. Lunch: 11. Last
Orders: 11. Credit Cards: Ac. Am. D. V. Seating Capacity: 100.
Veg. Parties (20).
The Chopstick Restaurant
244 Cowley Road. Tel: (0865) 725688
Dear Friends Chinese Restaurant
4 Woodstock Road. Tel: (0865) 54996
Elizabeth's Restaurant
84 St Aldates. Tel: (0865) 242230
The Gate of India Restaurant
High Street. Tel: (0865) 242062
Gee's Restaurant

61a Banbury Road. OX2 7DY Tel: (0865) 58346
Go Dutch
18 Park End Street. Tel: (0865) 240686
Hi-Lo Jamaican Eating House
70 Cowley Road. Tel: (0865) 725984
Jamaican Cuisine. Specialities: Vegetarian meals, goat, fish,
chicken, beef & pork dishes. Lunch: 1pm. Last Orders: Late.
House Wine: £ 4.50. Seating Capacity: 60. Banquets. Parties.
Weddings.
Jamal's Tandoori
108 Walton Street. Tel: (0865) 310102
Jomuna Tandoori Restaurant
240 Cowley Road. Tel: (0865) 251013
The Kashmir (Halal) Tandoori Restaurant
64 Cowley Road. Tel: (0865) 242941
Kentucky Fried Chicken
35 Cornmarket. Tel: (0865) 249300
The Kismet Restaurant
129a High Street. Tel: (0865) 2511150
Koto Brasserie
260 Banbury Road. Tel: (0865) 54117
La Capannina
247 Cowley Road. Tel: (0865) 248200
La Dolce Vita
215 Banbury Road. Tel: (0865) 53990
La Sorbonne Restaurant

THE 'BRIDGE OF SIGHS', HERTFORD COLLEGE, OXFORD

30a High Street. OX1 4DH Tel: (0865) 241320
Le Bistro du Marche
9A High Street. Tel: (0865) 723342
Liason Restaurant
29 Castle Street. Tel: (0865) 242944
Luna Caprese Restaurant
4 North Parade. Tel: (0865) 54812
Maxwells Restaurant
37 Queens Street. Tel: (0865) 242192
Michel's Brasserie
10 Little Clarendon Street. Tel: (0865) 52142
The Mitre
High Street. Tel: (0865) 244563
The Moonlight Restaurant
58 Cowley Road. Tel: (0865) 240275
Moti-Mahal Restaurant
86 St Clement's. Tel: (0865) 247093
The Nose Bag
6 St Michael's Street. Tel: (0865) 721033
The Old Parsonage Hotel
3 Banbury Road. Tel: (0865) 310310
The Opium Den
79 George Street. Tel: (0865) 248680
The Oxford Tandoori
209 Cowley Road. Tel: (0865) 241493
The Paddyfield Restaurant

39 Hythe Bridge Street. Tel: (0865) 248835
Pak Fook Chinese Restaurant
100 Cowley Road. Tel: (0865) 247958
Papa Chico
9B North Parade. Tel: (0865) 54911
Pasta Galore
103 Cowley Road. Tel: (0865) 722955
Pastifico Restaurant
14/16 George Street. Tel: (0865) 791032
Fresh Pasta and Pizza . Specialities: Veal, chicken and vegetarian specials. Lunch: 12am. Last Orders: 12pm. House Wine: £3.65. Credit Cards: Ac. V. Seating Capacity: 84. Veg. Wheelchair facilities. Parties.
The Peninsular Chinese Restaurant
21 George Street. Tel: (0865) 248224
Pizzaland
10 High Street. Tel: (0865) 724473
Pizzeria Mama Mia No 1
8 South Parade. Tel: (0865) 514141
The Polash Tandoori
25 Park End Street. Tel: (0865) 250244
The Poor Student Restaurant
1 Ship Street. Tel: (0865) 242317
Poppins Restaurant
29 George Street. Tel: (0865) 242735
The Prince of Bengal

MAGDALEN BRIDGE, OXFORD

92 Cowley Road. Tel: (0865) 241344
Raoul's Cocktail Bar
32 Walton Street. Tel: (0865) 53732
The Rick's Restaurant
146 Cowley Road. Tel: (0865) 251127
The Rimini Restaurant
97 St Clement's. Tel: (0865) 241158
Saraceno Ristorante
15 Magadelen Street. Tel: (0865) 249171
The Star of Asia
237 Cowley Road. Tel: (0865) 247798
Sweeny Todds
6 George Street. Tel: (0865) 723421
The Taj Mahal
16 Turl Street. Tel: (0865) 243783
Uddins Manzil Tandour Restaurant
123 Walton Street. Tel: (0865) 56153
Indian Cuisine. Specialities: Tandoori Chicken. Hours Open: Lunch: 12.00 - 3.00pm. Dinner: 6pm - Midnight. Last Orders: Midnight. Credit Cards: Ac. V. Seating Capacity: 45. Outdoor Eating. Vegetarian. Parties.
Wimpey
25 Cornmarket Street. Tel: (0865) 245151
The Wine Gallery
Concordia House, Blue Boar Street. Tel: (0865) 250440
Wing Ho Restaurant
133 Botley Road. Tel: (0865) 244454

PUBLIC HOUSES
The Anchor Inn
2 Hayfield Road. Tel: (0865) 510282
The Bakers Arms

Cardigan Street. Tel: (0865) 52310
The Bear Inn
Alfred St. Tel: (0865) 244680
Recommendations: Good Pub Guide.
The Berinsfield Arms
Tel: (0865) 340340
Berkshire House
Abingdon Road. Tel: (0865) 242423
Large roomy pub with large garden and play area. Good beer and food. Pub games including Aunt Sally.
Brewery: Morrells . Licensee: Mr Philip Plucknett. Opening Hours: 10.30 am - 11 pm. Food Available: 7 am - 7 pm. 3 Bedrooms: B&B per person: £11. Garden. Children's room.
The Black Swan
11 Crown Street. Tel: (0865) 242153
The Book Binders Arms
17 Victor Street. Tel: (0865) 53549
The Bricklayers Arms
Old Marston. Tel: (0865) 244575
The Bulldog
108 St Aldates. Tel: (0865) 250210
The Bullingdon Arms
Cowley Road. Tel: (0865) 244516
The Bystander
Besselsleigh Road, Sandleigh. Tel: (0895) 735234
The Carpenters Arms
Nelson Street. Tel: (0865) 510714
The Catherine Wheel
Tel: (0865) 890389
Chequers Inn
Tel: (0865) 891279
The Coach & Horses
St Clements. Tel: (0865) 243170
The Cricketers Arms
43 Ifley Road. Tel: (0865) 726264
The Dewdrop Inn
258 Banbury Road. Tel: (0865) 59372
The Dolly
Cornmarket. Tel: (0865) 244761
The Donnington Arms
Howard Street. Tel: (0865) 247342
The Duke of Cambridge
Little Clarendon Street. Tel: (0865) 53528
The Duke of Edinburgh
76 St Clement's. Tel: (0865) 247873
The Duke of Monmouth
260 Abingdon Road. Tel: (0865) 721612
The Duke of York
Norfolk Street. Tel: (0865) 248507
The Eagle & Child
Tel: (0865) 58085
The Eagle Tavern
Magdalen Road. Tel: (0865) 242091
The Fir Tree

Iffley Road. Tel: (0865) 247373
The Folly Bridge Inn
38 Abingdon Road. Tel: (0865) 790106
The Fox & Hounds
Abingdon Road. Tel: (0865) 722210
The Friar Bacon
Elsfield Way. Tel: (0865) 54198
The Gardeners Arms
Plantation Road. Tel: (0865) 59814
Recommendations: Good Pub Guide.
The Globe Inn
Cranham Street. Tel: (0865) 57759
The Gloucester Arms
Friars Entry. Tel: (0865) 241177
The Grapes
3 George Street. Tel: (0865) 247372
The Greyhound
Besselsleigh. Tel: (0865) 862110
The Harcourt Arms
Cranham Terrace Jericho. Tel: (0865) 53703
The Head of the River
Folly Bridge. Tel: (0865) 721600
The Hollybush Inn
Osney. Tel: (0865) 723454
The Horse & Jockey
69 Woodstock Road. Tel: (0865) 52719
Brewery: Morrells. Licensee: Mr M Timbs. Opening Hours: 11-
11pm. Food Available: 12 - 2 6 - 9pm. Garden. Children's area.
The Jack Russell
Salford Road, Old Marston. Tel: (0865) 247668
Licensee: Mr J MacDonald.
The Jericho Tavern
56 Walton Street. Tel: (0865) 54502
The Jolly Farmers
Paradise Street. Tel: (0865) 251165
The Jolly Postboys
22 Florence Park Road. Tel: (0865) 779307
The Kings Arms
283 Banbury Road. Tel: (0865) 54475
The Lamb & Flag Inn
St Giles. Tel: (0865) 515787
The Marlborough Arms
St Thomas Street. Tel: (0865) 243057
Marlborough House
60 Western Road. Tel: (0865) 243617
The Nags Head
Fisher Island. Tel: (0865) 249153
The Nelson
Cowley Centre. Tel: (0865) 777200
The New Inn
Cowley Road. Tel: (0865) 247519
Old Gatehouse of Oxford
Botley Road. OX2 0AB Tel: (0865) 242823
Old Tom Inn

ENTRANCE TO EXETER COLLEGE, OXFORD

St Aldgates. Tel: (0865) 243034
Olde Oxford Ale House
Paradise Street. Tel: (0865) 2505019
The Osney Arms
Botley Road. Tel: (0865) 247103
The Oxford Bakery & Brew House
14 Gloucester Street. Tel: (0865) 727265
Recommendations: Good Pub Guide.
The Oxford Blue
32 Marston Street. Tel: (0865) 723898
The Pennyfarthing
St Ebbes Street. Tel: (0865) 246007
The Perch
Binsey Lane. Tel: (0865) 240386
Recommendations: Good Pub Guide.
The Plasterers Arms
Marston Road. Tel: (0865) 247114
The Port Mahon
St Clements. Tel: (0865) 242338
The Prince of Wales
Charles Street. Tel: (0865) 241977
Brewery: Halls. Licensee: Mr J R Walsh. Opening Hours: 11 am
- 11 pm. Garden. Children's area.
The Queens Arms
1 Park End Street. Tel: (0865) 243253
Brewery: Morrells. Licensee: Mr R J Carter. Opening Hours: 11
am - 11 pm. 12 noon - 4 pm.

BICYCLES OUTSIDE LINCOLN COLLEGE, OXFORD

The Radcliffe Arms
Cranham Street. Tel: (0865) 52693
The Red Lion
Woodstock Road. Tel: (0865) 58598
The Red White & Blue
James Street. Tel: (0865) 247127
The Roebuck
8 Market Street. Tel: (0865) 248288
The Rose & Crown Public House
North Parade Avenue. Tel: (0865) 510551
The Royal Blenheim
St Ebbes. Tel: (0865) 248280
The Royal Greenjacket
Chester Street. Tel: (0865) 243230
The Royal Oak
42 Woodstock Road. Tel: (0865) 54230
The Shelley Arms
Cricket Road. Tel: (0865) 779309
Somerset House
241, Marston Road New Marston. Tel: (0865) 243687
Licensee: Mr P Wood.
The Star Royal
21 Rectory Road. Tel: (0865) 248011
The Temple Bar
21 Temple Street. Tel: (0865) 243251
The Turf Tavern
4 Bath Place Holywell. Tel: (0865) 243235
Recommendations: Good Pub Guide.
The University & City Arms
Cowley Road. Tel: (0865) 244386
The Victoria Arms
90 Walton Street. Tel: (0865) 57676
The Waterman's Arms
South Street, Osney. Tel: (0865) 248832
The Welsh Pony
George Street. Tel: (0865) 242998
The Westgate Public House
Tel: (0865) 250099
Wharf House
St Ebbes. Tel: (0865) 245070

The Wheatsheaf
High Street. Tel: (0865) 243276
The Woodstock Arms
272 Woodstock Road. Tel: (0865) 52454

TEA ROOMS
Beatons Sandwich Bar
77, The Market. Tel: (0865) 249527
Sandwich Bar/Café
Months Open: All year. Days Open: Monday - Saturday. Hours Open: 10-5. Wide range of made to order sandwiches, open sandwiches, bagels, filled croissants, pizza, wholefood savouries.
Browns Café
The Covered Market, Mitre Avenue. Tel: (0865) 243436
Chicken Barbeque
266 Cowley Road. Tel: (0865) 245891
Cornish Pastie Café
98 Rose Hill. Tel: (0865) 778028
Cripley Road Café
Station Approach, Botley Road. Tel: (0865) 728693
Crystal Snack Bar
107 Cowley Road. Tel: (0865) 241577
The Excelsior Café
250 Cowley Road. Tel: (0865) 248504
George's Café
77 The Market. Tel: (0865) 249527
Le Papillon Coffee House
35 Castle Street. Tel: (0865) 249410
Munchy Munchy Food Bar
6 Park End Street. Tel: (0865) 245710
Queens Lane Coffee House
40 High Street. Tel: (0865) 240082
The Rosie Lee
51 High Street. Tel: (0865) 244429
St Giles Café
52 St Giles. Tel: (0865) 52110
The Wykeham Coffee Shop
15 Holywell. Tel: (0865) 246916

OTHER AMENITIES
ART GALLERIES
Art Et Cetera
127, Walton St. Tel: (0865) 513916
Chinese Art Centre
50, High Street. Tel: (0865) 242167
Art Gallery
Months Open: All Year. Days Open: All week. Hours Open: 10 am - 5.30 pm (weekdays) 2 - 5pm (Sundays). Open Bank Holidays. Proprietor: Gordon Aldrick..
City Gallery
15, Cowley Road. Tel: (0865) 790402
Magna Gallery
41, High Street. Tel: (0865) 245805
Oxford Gallery Ltd

23, High Street. Tel: (0865) 242731

Oxford Print Shops

46c, Richmond Road. Tel: (0865) 56099

Selling prints and paintings of Oxford
Months Open: All Year. Days Open: Tuesday to Sunday. Hours
Open: 10.30 am - 5 pm Tuesday to Saturday. 11 am - 5 pm
Sundays. Closed Bank Holidays. Prints of Oxford by well known
artists, unframed, framed and framed to order. A beautiful
selection in a quaint old stone courtyard. Rates: From about £1
to £75. Proprietor: F J O Mahony.

Sanders of Oxford Ltd

104, High Street. Tel: (0865) 242590

Antique prints, maps and book sellers
Months Open: All year. Days Open: Monday to Saturday.
Hours Open: 9 am - 1 pm 2.15 - 5.15pm Weekdays. 9am - 1pm
Saturdays. Closed Bank Holiday. Proprietor: Barbara Macleod.

BOAT HIRE

Boat Enquiries Ltd

43, Botley Road. Tel: (0865) 727288

College Cruisers Ltd

Combe Road Wharf, Combe Road. OX2 6BL
Tel: (0865) 54343

Hubbucks Boat Hire

2, Folly Bridge. OX1 4LB Tel: (0865) 722426/244235

Medley Boat Station

Port Meadow, End of Waltonwell Road.
Tel: (0865) 511660

Orchard Cruisers (Oxford) Ltd

Castle Mill Boatyard, Cardigan Street. Tel: (0865) 54043

Salter Bros Ltd

Folly Bridge. Tel: (0865) 243421

BUS & COACH SERVICES

Thames Transit Ltd

Horspath Road. OX4 2RY Tel: (0865) 747879

CAR HIRE

A J Webb

445, Cowley Road. Tel: (0865) 778255

Baldwin Car Hire

63, Cherwell Drive. OX3 0ND Tel: (0865) 247478

Cliff Cars

49, Sunderland Avenue. Tel: (0865) 58960

D Atherton

153 Cummor Road, Wootton, Boars Hill.
Tel: (0865) 739967

Luxicars (hire) Ltd

108, St Aldates. Tel: (0865) 241641

MJM

103, Walton Street. Tel: (0865) 514168

Steve Cars

19, Green Street. Tel: (0865) 246214

Whites of Oxford

53, Stanway Road, Risinghurst. OX3 8HU
Tel: (0865) 61265

CAR HIRE/SELF DRIVE

TRINITY COLLEGE, OXFORD

Barclay of Oxford

Barclay House, Botley Road. Tel: (0865) 722444

Months Open: All year. Days Open: All week. Hours Open:
8.30am - 5.30pm. Fiat and Mitsubishi dealers. Self-drive hire
cars. Sales, service and parts facilities. Proprietor: R G Bentley.

Bratt Vehicle Hire

395, Cowley Road. Tel: (0865) 715145

Godfrey Davis Europcar Ltd

Seacourt Tower, Botley Road. Tel: (0865) 246373

Open all year. Open: Monday to Saturday. Hours : 8.30 - 5.30
Monday to Friday 8.30 - 12.30 Saturday. Open Bank Holidays.
Van hire: Small Escort, transits, Renault Traffic, Luton Box
van, Renault Master. Leasehire: Minilease. Continental: Guar-
anteed Superdrive Sterling. Inclusive rate Weekend (3 days Fri-
Mon) from £43 inclusive. Rates: Local hire from £26 allinclu-
sive, insurance VAT no mileage. One way 24 hours hire from £35
all inclusive, VAT no mileage. Proprietor: Lisa Cameron.

Hotsons Hire (Oxford) Ltd

332, Abingdon Road. Tel: (0865) 241857

Humphries

72, Rose Hill. Tel: (0865) 774696

Salters of Oxford Ltd

281, Banbury Road. Tel: (0865) 512277

Shamrock Cars

195, Divinity Road. Tel: (0865) 723890

Swan National Rentals Ltd

St Clement's Garage, Dawson Street. Tel: (0865) 240471

CARAVAN PARKS

Oxford Camping International

426, Abingdon Road. Tel: (0865) 246551

CINEMAS

Cannon

George Street. Tel: (0865) 244607

Penultimate Picture Palace

Jeune St. Tel: (0865) 723837

Phoenix 1 and 2
57, Walton Street. Tel: (0865) 54909
STORES
Boswell & Co
1, Broad Street. Tel: (0865) 241244
British Home Stores
9, St Ebbes. Tel: (0865) 728828
C & A
Westgate. Tel: (0865) 721466
Clarendon Shopping Centre
Clarendon Centre, Shoe Lane. Tel: (0865) 251493
Debenhams Plc
Magdalen Street. Tel: (0865) 243161
Littlewoods
52/53, Cornmarket Street. Tel: (0865) 244781
Marks & Spencers Plc
Queen Street. Tel: (0865) 248075
Miss Selfridge Ltd
27, Westgate. Tel: (0865) 240739
Next Plc
4th Avenue, The Covered Market. Tel: (0865) 247919
Selfridges
Westgate. Tel: (0865) 244991
GARDEN CENTRES
B & Q
John Allen Centre, Between Towns Road. Tel: (0865) 749339
Summertown Garden Centre
200-202, Banbury Road. OX2 7BY Tel: (0865) 54956
HEALTH CLUBS
Charlton Club
36-39 , Park End Street. OX1 1JD Tel: (0865) 243584
Clive Parkinson's Martial Arts and Fitness Centre
193, Cowley Road. Tel: (0865) 251428
Inshape Body Studios Ltd
6/7, High Street. Tel: (0865) 251261
Oxford Health Club c/o Oxford Rowing Club
Meadow Lane, Donnington Bridge Road.
Tel: (0865) 247716
HOLIDAY ACCOMODATION
Groveson Holiday Homes
24, George Street. Tel: (0865) 245454
HOSPITALS
Acland Hospital
25, Banbury Road. Tel: (0865) 52081
Nuffield Hospital
25, Banbury Road. Tel: (0865) 52081
Nuffield Nursing Homes Trust
25, Banbury Road. Tel: (0865) 54261
Oxford Eye Hospital
Woodstock Road. Tel: (0865) 249891
Priory Clinic at Oxford
23, Banbury Road. Tel: (0865) 56097

Radcliffe Infirmary
Woodstock Road. Tel: (0865) 249891
Rivermead Rehabilitation Centre
Abingdon Road. Tel: (0865) 240321
Warneford Hospital
Tel: (0865) 245651
LEISURE CENTRES
Douglas Bader Sports Centre
Woodstock Road. Tel: (0865) 53547
East Oxford Games Hall
5, Collins Street. Tel: (0865) 242486
MUSEUMS
British Telecom
35, Speedwell Street. Tel: (0865) 246601
Heritage Projects (Oxford) Ltd
33-35 George Street. Tel: (0865) 728822
NIGHT CLUBS
Bogarts
15a, St Clement's. Tel: (0865) 241047
Boodles Night Club
35, Westgate. Tel: (0865) 245136
Months Open: All year. Days Open: Monday - Tuesday for private hire ,Wednesday - Saturday open to the public. Hours Open: 9.00 pm - 2.00 am. Available for private hire on Bank Holidays. Wednesday - Party night .Thursday - Ladies night. Friday - Promotional night. Saturday - Big night out. Proprietor: Mark Thurlow.
RAILWAY STATION
Oxford Parcels and Red Star
Tel: (0865) 2455444
Oxford Travel Centre
Tel: (0865) 722333
SKATING RINKS
Oxford Ice Rink
Oxpens Road. Tel: (0865) 247676
SNOOKER CENTRE
Beckley Club
36-39, Park End Street. OX1 1JD Tel: (0865) 250181
SPORTS CLUBS
Action Sport
5, Collins Street. Tel: (0865) 242486
Blackfriars Athletic F C Sports & Social Club
228, Botley Road. Tel: (0865) 241311
Christians in Sport
7, St Aldgates. Tel: (0865) 240407
City of Oxford Rowing Club
Donnington Bridge. Tel: (0865) 242576
East Oxford Bowls Club
285, Cowley Road. Tel: (0865) 249760
Norham Gardens Lawn Tennis Club
Benson Place. Tel: (0865) 54136
Oxford Boys Club
Marston Ferry Road. Tel: (0865) 52813
Oxford City F C Supporters Club

THE EXQUISITE TRACERY OF CHRIST CHURCH COLLEGE, OXFORD

Abingdon Road. Tel: (0865) 242439
Oxford City Football Club
Whitehouse Road. Tel: (0865) 248391
Oxford Rugby Club
Southern By Pass. Tel: (0865) 243984
South Oxford Bowls Club
Sunningwell Road. Tel: (0865) 243129
Stripes Pool Club

190, Cowley Road. Tel: (0865) 721881
Temple Martial Arts Kung Fu Club
193, Cowley Road. Tel: (0865) 251428
SPORTS TRAINING
Taishi Martial Arts
70, St Clements. Tel: (0865) 791999
THEATRES
Apollo Theatre

91

CHRIST CHURCH, OXFORD

George Street. Tel: (0865) 244544
Old Fire Station Arts Centre
40, George Street. Tel: (0865) 722648
Pegasus Theatre
Magdalen Road. Tel: (0865) 722851
Playhouse
Beaumont Street. Tel: (0865) 247134
TOURIST OFFICE
Oxford Information Centre
St Aldates. Tel: (0865) 726871
TOURS AND SIGHTS
Japanese Connection
38, Walton Street. Tel: (0865) 511872
Whites of Oxford
53, Stanway Road, Risinghurst. OX3 8HU
Tel: (0865) 61265
UNIVERSITIES/COLLEGES
All Souls' College
High Street. Tel: (0865) 279379
Balliol College
Broad Street. Tel: (0865) 277777
Brasenose College
Radcliffe Square. Tel: (0865) 277830
Campion Hall
Brewer Street. Tel: (0865) 240861
Christ Church
St Aldgates. Tel: (0865) 276150
Corpus Christi College
Merton Street. Tel: (0865) 276700
Greyfriars Hall
Iffley Road. Tel: (0865) 243694
Hertford College

Catte Street. Tel: (0865) 279400
Jesus College
Turl Street. Tel: (0865) 279700
Keble College
8, Norham Gardens. Tel: (0865) 53909
Lady Margaret Hall
Norham Gardens. Tel: (0865) 274300
Lincoln College
Turl Street. Tel: (0865) 279800
Magdalen College
High Street. Tel: (0865) 276000
Manchester College
Tel: (0865) 241514
Mansfield College
Mansfield Road. Tel: (0865) 270999
Merton College
Merton Street. Tel: (0865) 276310
New College
Longwall Street. Tel: (0865) 248451
Nuffield College
New Road. Tel: (0865) 278500
Oriel College
The Porters Lodge, Oriel Square. Tel: (0865) 276555
Pembroke College
Pembroke Square. Tel: (0865) 276444
Queen's College
High Street. Tel: (0865) 279121
Regent's Park College
Pusey Street. Tel: (0865) 59887
Somerville College
Woodstock Road. Tel: (0865) 270600
St Anne's College

Woodstock Road. Tel: (0865) 274800
St Anthony's College
Woodstock Road. Tel: (0865) 59651
St Benet's Hall
38, St Giles. Tel: (0865) 515006
St Catherine's College
Manor Road. Tel: (0865) 271700
St Cross College
St Giles. Tel: (0865) 278490
St Edmund Hall
Queens Lane. Tel: (0865) 279000
St Hilda's College
Cowley Place. Tel: (0865) 242170
St Hugh's College
St Margrets Road. Tel: (0865) 274900
St John's College
St Giles. Tel: (0865) 247671
St Peter's College
New Inn, Hall Street. Tel: (0865) 278900
Trinity College
Broad Street. Tel: (0865) 279900
University College
25, Staverton Road. Tel: (0865) 54993
University College Oxford
High Street. Tel: (0865) 241661
University of Oxford
Cross Road. Tel: (0865) 270000
Wadham College
Parks Road. Tel: (0865) 271481
Warnborough College
Boars Hill. Tel: (0865) 277900
Wolfson College
Linton Road. Tel: (0865) 274100
Worcester College
Walton Street. Tel: (0865) 54710
Wine Gallery
Concordia House, Blue Boar Street. Tel: (0865) 250440
WINE BARS
Bacchus Wine Bar
29, George Street. Tel: (0865) 241127
Crypt
Frewin Court, Cornmarket Street. Tel: (0865) 251000

MERCURY, TOM QUAD, CHRIST CHURCH, OXFORD

Emperors Wine Bar
22, Broad Street. Tel: (0865) 723642
Set
Victoria Court, George Street. Tel: (0865) 728554
YOUTH HOSTELS
Church Housing Association
8, Speedwell Street. Tel: (0865) 243071
St Gregory & St Macrina House
1, Canterbury Court. Tel: (0865) 54844
YWCA
Clarendon Centre, Cornmarket Street.
Tel: (0865) 726110

MERTON FIELD. OXFORD

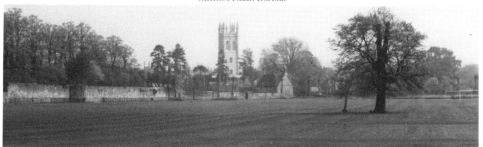

THE WEIR AT PANGBOURNE

PANGBOURNE

This delightful Thames-side town, with its spectacular weir, has associations with Kenneth Grahame, who wrote 'The Wind in the Willows'; the illustrations by E.H.Shepherd were based on this beautiful stretch of the river. The river here is absolutely breathtaking as it cuts through the steep woody hills from the Goring Gap upstream. Brunel's Great Western Railway speeds through, and there is an active toll bridge taking motorists across the Thames from the Berkshire bank to Whitchurch. The church has a brightly coloured pinnacled brick tower, and is opposite the house where Kenneth Grahame lived and worked. Pangbourne College, founded in 1917 by Sir Thomas Devitt, stands at the top of a steep hill; it was used to train boys for a career in the Merchant Navy. On the Wallingford road there is a row of Edwardian villas overlooking the river known locally as 'the Seven Deadly Sins '.

Population: 2,505. Early closing: Thursday. Map Ref: H 14.

CHURCH
St James

HOTELS
The Copper Inn
Church Road. Tel: (073 57) 2244
The Star Inn
Reading Road. Tel: (073 57) 2566
Ye Old George Hotel
The Square. RG8 7AJ Tel: (073 57) 2237

PUBLIC HOUSES
The Cross Keys
Church Road. Tel: (07357) 3268
The Swan
Shooters Hill. Tel: (07357) 4494

OTHER AMENITIES
CAR HIRE/SELF DRIVE
Pangbourne Ford

63/65, Reading Road. Tel: (07357) 4461
GARDEN CENTRE
Percy Stone Limited
4-10 Reading Road. RG8 7LY Tel: (07357) 2111
LEISURE CENTRE
Drakes Centre
Pangbourne College. Tel: (07357) 4988
RAILWAY STATION
Pangbourne Station
Shooters Hill. Tel: (07357) 2927
WINE BAR
Ducks Ditty
11, Reading Road. Tel: (07357) 3050

🍺 🍺 🍺 🍺 🍺 🍺 🍺

PEPPARD COMMON
Map Ref: J 13.

HOTEL
The Red Lion
RG9 5LB Tel: (049 17) 329

🍺 🍺 🍺 🍺 🍺 🍺 🍺

PISHILL
Population: 288. Map Ref: K 12.

CHURCH
Dedication unknown.
There was a small plain Norman church here which was replaced in 1854.

PUBLIC HOUSE
The Crown
Tel: (049 163) 364
Recommendations: Good Pub Guide.

🍺 🍺 🍺 🍺 🍺 🍺 🍺

POSTCOMBE
Map Ref: J 13.

RESTAURANT
The Rickshaw Inn
London Road. Tel: (084428) 213

🍺 🍺 🍺 🍺 🍺 🍺 🍺

PUSEY
There is a legend in the village that the land was presented by King Canute to one of the Pusey family in gratitude for a warning of a murderous ambush. The greystone village is grouped around

the present Pusey House built in 1753.
Population: 53. Map Ref: C 10.

PLACES OF INTEREST
Pusey House and Gardens
Tel: (036787) 222
15 acres of one of the great gardens of England. Wonderful herbaceous borders, a walled garden, a water garden with Chinese bridge. The house is not open to the public.
Months Open: Easter Saturday - October. Days Open: Daily except Monday and Friday. Hours Open: 2-6. Bank Holidays: Open Bank Holiday Monday.

CHURCH
All Saints
Built for Jane Pusey, to whom there is a monument inside the church. The three principle windows are Venetian, as are the screens between the chapels and the nave.

ఇ ఇ ఇ ఇ ఇ ఇ ఇ

PYRTON
Map Ref: J 10.

PUBLIC HOUSE
The Plough
Tel: (049161) 2003

ఇ ఇ ఇ ఇ ఇ ఇ ఇ

RADCOT
Radcot Bridge is one of the oldest bridges on the Thames, and as such was an important crossing-point on the road to the Royalist garrison in Faringdon. During the Civil War it was the scene of several skirmishes. The settlement consists of the Manor House, also a Royalist stronghold, which lay down its arms to the Parliamentarians, an inn and the bridge itself.
Map Ref: B 9.

PUBLIC HOUSE
The Swan Hotel
Radcot Bridge. Tel: (036781) 220
Recommendations: Good Pub Guide.

ఇ ఇ ఇ ఇ ఇ ఇ ఇ

RADLEY
Radley is best known for its public school which was founded in 1874 by Dr Sewell in a Georgian manor house which used to be owned by the Bowyer (sausages) family.
Map Ref: F 10.

CHURCH
St James

PUBLIC HOUSE
The Bowyer Arms
Tel: (0235) 23452
Brewery: Morlands. Licensee: Mr E Lumb. Opening Hours: 11.30am - 3 pm . 6 pm - 11 pm. Food Available: Lunch and early evening. Four Bedrooms: B&B per person: £12.50. Garden. Childrens area.

OTHER AMENITIES
CARAVAN PARKS
Bigwood Caravan Park
Sugworth Lane. Tel: (0865) 735168
Lower Radley Park
Park Farm. Tel: (0235) 21279

ఇ ఇ ఇ ఇ ఇ ఇ ఇ

RADNAGE
Map Ref: K 10.

PUBLIC HOUSE
The Three Horseshoes
Bennett End Road. Tel: (024026) 3273

ఇ ఇ ఇ ఇ ఇ ఇ ఇ

RAMSDEN
North of Witney, this is an attractive village with one street containing neat houses and an Elizabethan house. The village became a parish in 1857 when Wychwood Forest was disafforested by an Act of Parliament, and the church was then built.
Population: 380. Map Ref: C 6.

CHURCH
St James

PUBLIC HOUSE
The Stag & Hounds
Main Street. Tel: (099 386) 278

OTHER AMENITIES
GARDEN CENTRE
Hilltop Garden Centre and Nursery
Witney Road   (B4022). OX7 3AS Tel: (099 386) 403

ఇ ఇ ఇ ఇ ఇ ఇ ఇ

REMENHAM
On the main A423 into Henley-on-Thames, Remenham is a small hamlet set in undulating

woodland in a pretty part of England.
Map Ref: K 13.

PUBLIC HOUSE
The Little Angel
Remenham Lane. Tel: (0491) 574165
NIGHT CLUB
Bensons
Remenham Hill. Tel: (0491) 575430

🐦 🐦 🐦 🐦 🐦 🐦 🐦

ROTHERFIELD GREYS
Population: 344. Map Ref: J 13.

PUBLIC HOUSES
The Dog Inn
Peppard Common. Tel: (04917) 343
The Malsters
Tel: (04917) 400

🐦 🐦 🐦 🐦 🐦 🐦 🐦

ROTHERFIELD PEPPARD
Population: 1,368. Map Ref: J 13.

PUBLIC HOUSE
The Unicorn Public House
Colemore Lane. Tel: (04917) 452

TEA ROOMS
Carmen's Cafe
Wantage Road. Tel: (0235) 831832

🐦 🐦 🐦 🐦 🐦 🐦 🐦

RUSSELLS WATER
Map Ref: J 12.

PUBLIC HOUSE
Beehive Inn
Tel: (0491) 641306
Recommendations: Good Pub Guide.

🐦 🐦 🐦 🐦 🐦 🐦 🐦

SALFORD
On the A44 to Moreton-in-Marsh, Salford has an attractive rectory and a Norman church.
Map Ref: B 4.

CHURCH
St Mary

PUBLIC HOUSE
The Cross Hands Inn
Tel: (0608) 3106

🐦 🐦 🐦 🐦 🐦 🐦 🐦

SANDFORD ST MARTIN
A peaceful manorial ironstone village, with the River Dorn flowing through it, with church, manor house and Sandford Park.
Population: 200. Map Ref: E 4.

CHURCH
St Martin
A 13th century church restored in 1856 by G E Street.

🐦 🐦 🐦 🐦 🐦 🐦 🐦

SANDFORD-ON-THAMES
Map Ref: G9.
CHURCH
St Andrew
An essentially Norman church; the south and east walls are original, as is the chancel window. There were major Victorian renovations.

PUBLIC HOUSES
The Catherine Wheel
Tel: (0895) 778340
The Fox
Henley Road. Tel: (0865) 777803
The Kings Arms
Tel: (0865) 777095

OTHER AMENITIES
CARAVAN PARK
Temple Court Country Club Ltd
Henley Road. Tel: (0865) 779359

🐦 🐦 🐦 🐦 🐦 🐦 🐦

SHENINGTON
A lovely village with a large green surrounded by golden stone houses and an inn dated 1700. The church has an early Tudor tower.
Population: 356. Map Ref: D 1.

CHURCH
Holy Trinity

PUBLIC HOUSE
The Bell Inn
Tel: (029587) 274

SHILLINGFORD BRIDGE

SHILLINGFORD

A small settlement on the Thames with an elegant bridge and an impressive looking hotel which overlooks it.

Map Ref: H 11.

HOTEL
Shillingford Bridge Hotel

OX10 8LZ Tel: (0867) 328567

This hotel is situated on a beautiful reach of theThames, with a quarter mile frontage.

🐦 🐦 🐦 🐦 🐦 🐦 🐦

SHILTON

A lovely village situated in a valley formed by the Shill brook. There is a Jacobean house near to the ford, and Manor Farm beyond which has an old dovecote.

Population: 450. Map Ref: B 8.

CHURCH
Holy Rood

The church has Norman arches and 14th century carvings of the Passion on the font. The 'rood' or cross was replaced during 1884-8.

PUBLIC HOUSE
The Rose & Crown

OX8 4AB Tel: (0993) 842280

🐦 🐦 🐦 🐦 🐦 🐦 🐦

SHIPLAKE

On the banks of the Thames, Shiplake has a church, where Alfred Tennyson was married in 1850, a vicarage and Shiplake Court, now Shiplake College, a public school. Lower Shiplake developed around the station.

Population: 2,015. Map Ref: K 14.

CHURCH
St Peter & St Paul

Yet another restoration by G E Street of 1869, which amounted to a rebuilding.

PUBLIC HOUSE
The Flowing Spring

Tel: (0734) 693207

Recommendations: Good Pub Guide.

🐦 🐦 🐦 🐦 🐦 🐦 🐦

SHIPPON

Map Ref: F 10.

GUEST HOUSE
Old Vicarage

Barrow Road. Tel: (0235) 30891

PUBLIC HOUSE
The Prince of Wales

Barrow Road. Tel: (0235) 20845

🐦 🐦 🐦 🐦 🐦 🐦 🐦

SHIPTON-ON-CHERWELL

A Victorian church rebuilt in 1831, a manor house

whose core dates back to 16th century, and an old rectory comprise this small settlement.

Map Ref: F 6.

RESTAURANT

Little Chef

Banbury Road. Tel: (086 75) 71475

🐾 🐾 🐾 🐾 🐾 🐾 🐾

SHIPTON-UNDER-WYCHWOOD

Situated in the once Royal Forest of Wychwood, this village has an interesting parish church, and many fine old houses and hostelries. Restored Shipton Court is one of the finest Jacobean buildings in the village (although not open to the public) and the fountain is dedicated to 19 men from the village who perished in a shipwreck in 1874. There is an old-established flour mill which produces a flour called Cotswold crunch.

Population: 1,087. Early closing: Wednesday. Map Ref: B 6.

CHURCH
St Mary

A double-aisled church with an elegant 13th century spire.

HOTELS

The Lamb Inn

High Street. OX7 6DQ Tel: (0993) 830465

Traditional Cotswold stone inn set on the edge of a pretty village, renowned for its cuisine and cottagey atmosphere. *BEDROOMS: 3 Double, (3 en suite, 3 TV, 3 tea/coffee) 2 Twin, (2 en suite, 2 TV, 2 tea/coffee) RESTAURANT: English Cuisine. Lunch: £ 7.75. Dinner: £ 13.50. House Wine: £ 6.00. Credit Cards: AC. AM. D. V.*

Weekend Breaks: 2 nights: £ 32.50. 3 nights: £ 45.00.

The Shaven Crown Hotel

High Street. OX7 6BA Tel: (0993) 830330

OTHER AMENITIES

TOURS AND SIGHTS

Guys Tours

Gales Green, High Street. Tel: (0993) 831532

🐾 🐾 🐾 🐾 🐾 🐾 🐾

SIBFORD GOWER

A rustic village with cottages and duckponds. There is a meeting house and a manor house that was rebuilt in 1915.

Population: 455. Map Ref: D 2.

CHURCH
Holy Trinity

PUBLIC HOUSES

The Bishop Blaize Inn

Burdrop. Tel: (029 578) 321

The Wykham Arms

Tel: (029 578) 351

🐾 🐾 🐾 🐾 🐾 🐾 🐾

SOULDERN

A picturesque village on the Northamptonshire border once visited by Willam Wordsworth, who was so delighted by the place that he was inspired to write 'A Parsonage in Oxfordshire' in appreciation. The village still has much charm, set, as it is, against a wooded park which runs beside the Ockley Brook.

Map Ref: G 4.

CHURCH
St Mary

The tower of this small church is Norman, and more was added in the 12th century. There was a restoration in 1906, using old materials.

HOTEL

The Fox Inn

Fox Lane. Tel: (086 96) 284

Traditional Cotswold stone country inn in idyllic village. Its location makes the Fox Inn the ideal base for the Cotswolds, Oxford, Stratford, Warwick and Silverstone. *BEDROOMS: 3 Double, (2 en suite, 3 TV, 3 tea/coffee) B&B £25.00 - £ 32.50. 1 Twin, (1 TV, 1 tea/coffee) RESTAURANT: European Cuisine. Lunch: £ 5.00. Dinner: £ 10.00. House Wine: £ 3.95. À La Carte: £ 7.50. Specialities: Roast Sunday Lunch £5.75. Sports Facilities: Golf.*

Weekend Breaks: 2 nights: £ 35.00.

PUBLIC HOUSE

The Bear Inn

Tel: (08696) 6785

Free House. Licensee: Mr K Clifford. Opening Hours: 11.30am - 2.30pm 6.30 - 11pm. Food Available: 12 -2 pm 7 - 9pm Except Sundays. Garden. Childrens area on Sundays.

🐾 🐾 🐾 🐾 🐾 🐾 🐾

SOUTH HINKSEY

A suburb of Oxford now, which still manages to retain a village atmosphere around the 13th century church.

Population: 344. Map Ref: E 9.

CHURCH
St Lawrence

GUEST HOUSE
Cotmore D E J
12 Manor Road. Tel: (0865) 739980

PUBLIC HOUSE
The General Elliot
Manor Road. Tel: (0865) 739369

OTHER AMENITIES
GARDEN CENTRE
Johnsons Garden Centre
Southern ByPass. Tel: (0865) 730368

᪐᪐ ᪐᪐ ᪐᪐ ᪐᪐ ᪐᪐ ᪐᪐ ᪐᪐

SOUTH LEIGH
A tiny farming village. John Wesley preached his very first sermon here when he was 21 in 1725. *Map Ref: D 8.*

CHURCHES
Methodist Chapel
St James
15th century church noted for its wall paintings which were restored in the 19th century.

PUBLIC HOUSE
The Masons Arms
Tel: (0993) 702485
Recommendations: Good Pub Guide.

᪐᪐ ᪐᪐ ᪐᪐ ᪐᪐ ᪐᪐ ᪐᪐ ᪐᪐

SOUTH MORETON
A village with a wide main street leading to a Georgian house. There is an old mill and farmyard and a prehistoric mound next to the church. *Population: 334. Map Ref: G 12.*

CHURCH
St John Baptist

᪐᪐ ᪐᪐ ᪐᪐ ᪐᪐ ᪐᪐ ᪐᪐ ᪐᪐

SOUTH NEWINGTON
On the River Swere, with an interesting church. *Population: 291. Map Ref: D 3.*

CHURCH
St Peter ad Vincula
Medieval wall paintings including Thomas a Becket 's martyrdom, Christ carrying the Cross, the Crucifixion and the Resurrection. Attracts many visitors.

PUBLIC HOUSE
The Wykham Arms
Tel: (0295) 721166

᪐᪐ ᪐᪐ ᪐᪐ ᪐᪐ ᪐᪐ ᪐᪐ ᪐᪐

SPARSHOLT
An unspoilt village situated in a fairly wooded area below the Downs near Wantage. *Population: 272. Map Ref: C 11.*

CHURCH
Holy Cross
There has been a church here since the Norman Conquest and the present one has a 14th century chancel. There are three 14th century effigies, unusual for their giant size and for being made of oak.

PUBLIC HOUSE
The Star Inn
Tel: (023 559) 247

᪐᪐ ᪐᪐ ᪐᪐ ᪐᪐ ᪐᪐ ᪐᪐ ᪐᪐

STADHAMPTON
A large village in the Thames valley with a village green and a 17th century manor house. Thomas Dormer built a large house in 1660 which was burnt down soon after; all that remains are the gatepiers and an avenue. *Population: 697. Map Ref: H 10.*

CHURCH
St John Baptist
The church has a tower with four Georgian urns on top, but is much rebuilt.

᪐᪐ ᪐᪐ ᪐᪐ ᪐᪐ ᪐᪐ ᪐᪐ ᪐᪐

STANDLAKE
A half-timbered village with a manor house remaining in the village street and a 13th century church. There are gravel pits around the village, one of which has become part of a leisure centre, and another a Nature Reserve. *Population: 1,257. Map Ref: D 9.*

CHURCHES
Methodist Chapel
St Giles

PUBLIC HOUSE
The Black Horse
Tel: (086731) 307

THE GREAT KITCHEN, STANTON HARCOURT MANOR

OTHER AMENITIEIES

CARAVAN PARKS
Hardwick Parks Ltd
Caravan and Camping Park, Downs Road. OX8 7TV
Tel: (086731) 501 or (0993) 775272
Lincoln Farm Park
High Street. OX8 7RH Tel: (086731) 239

PUBLIC HOUSES

The Anchor Inn
High Street. Tel: (03677) 325
The Horse & Jockey
25 Faringdon Road. Tel: (03677) 302
The Red Lion Inn
19 High Street. Tel: (03677) 258

🐾 🐾 🐾 🐾 🐾 🐾 🐾

🐾 🐾 🐾 🐾 🐾 🐾 🐾

STANFORD-IN-THE-VALE

A picturesque village which was once the substantial market centre of the Vale of the White Horse. Its importance declined over the years, but it still has some large houses along the road from Lower Green, past Church Green to Upper Green. Stanford too suffered during the Civil War as troops of both sides foraged for food, and Cromwell's men looted the Manor House, failing to find the valuables which were so well hidden that they weren't discovered till 1825.
Map Ref: C 11.

CHURCH
St Denys
This large church is dedicated, unusually, to St Denys, the patron saint of France. The saint's finger was supposed to have been kept here, and was displayed from time to time to the villagers.

STANTON HARCOURT

This village is situated near the confluence of the rivers Thames and Windrush, and is centred around the church, the Manor House and the splendid 17th century parsonage.
Population: 758. Map Ref: D 8.

PLACES OF INTEREST
Stanton Harcourt Manor
Tel: (0865) 881928
Medieval buildings nine miles from Oxford. The Harcourt family occupied the Manor House since the 12th century, but the house was almost entirely demolished in 1750 when they moved to to Nuneham.* Of the remains, Pope's Tower is so called because Alexander Pope worked on his translation of the Illiad there (he scratched his name on one of the windowpanes). The Great Kitchen, one of the few medieval kitchens to survive, has no chimney; the smoke from the ovens and fires would collect in the cone of the roof and be extracted through wooden louvres. Stanton

ROUSHAM HOUSE

Harcourt Manor has 15 acres of garden and is open to the public. *See Nuneham Courtney.
Months Open: April-September. Days Open: Ring for exact days. Hours Open: 2-5pm. Bank Holidays: Open.

CHURCH
St Michael
The church is an excellent example of Norman and Early English. The Harcourt monuments and tombs range from the standardbearer for Henry Tudor at Bosworth Field in 1485, to Sir William Harcourt, who was Chancellor of the Exchequer to Gladstone. The wooden chancel screen is almost certainly one of the oldest in England.

HOTEL
The Harcourt Arms
OX8 1RJ Tel: (0865) 881931
A 17th Century Inn featuring inglenook fireplaces.

🐿 🐿 🐿 🐿 🐿 🐿 🐿

STANTON ST JOHN

Mostly owned by New College, Oxford, Stanton St John is an attractive stone village to the west of Oxford. Opposite the church is an old house where John White lived, who founded the Massachusetts Company which sent settlers to start a new colony in the USA.
Population: 418. Map Ref: H 8.

CHURCH
St John Baptist
Set on a mound in the centre of the village, from where there are superb views to the distant Chilterns; it has an Early English chancel and some medieval glass.

PUBLIC HOUSES
The George
Tel: (086735) 648
The Star Inn
Tel: (086735) 277

🐿 🐿 🐿 🐿 🐿 🐿 🐿

STEEPLE ASTON

The largest of the three Astons, there are some fine houses and high stone walls.
Population: 869. Early closing: Saturday. Map Ref: F 5.

PLACES OF INTEREST
Rousham House
Tel: (0869) 47110
An imposing 17th century castellated house with notable gardens created by William Kent in 1738, one of the few man-made landscapes of its time to have survived intact. It was a Royalist garrison in the Civil War.
Months Open: Garden: All Year. House: April- September . Days Open: Garden: Daily. House: Wednesday and Sunday. Hours Open: Garden: 10am-4.30pm. House: 2-4.30pm. Bank Holidays: Bank Holiday Monday 2-4.30pm.

CHURCHES
St Peter
A mixture of dates and styles. The famous 14th century Steeple Aston cope, a needlework masterpiece, is now in the Victoria and Albert Museum.
Victory Baptist Church
Fir Lane. Tel: (0869) 40892

HOTEL
Hopcrofts Holt Hotel
Banbury Road. OX5 3QQ Tel: (0869) 40259
Originally a 16th century coaching inn, the hotel has recently been extended to provide excellent modern amenities and yet retains its original charm.
BEDROOMS: 11 Single, (11 en suite, 11 TV, 11 phone, 11 tea/coffee) 34 Double, (34 en suite, 34 TV, 34 phone, 34 tea/coffee) 19 Twin, (19 en suite, 19 TV, 19 phone, 19 tea/coffee) RESTAURANT: English/French Cuisine. Lunch: £ 8.25. Dinner: £ 12.00. House Wine: £ 7.25. À La Carte: £ 12.00. HOTEL INFORMATION: CF. W. B. F. 150 space Car Park. Dogs. Credit Cards: AC. AM. D. V. Recommendations: AA**. ER. Weekend Breaks: 2 nights: £ 64.00. 3 nights: £ 96.00. Allowance towards dinner: £ 12.00.

PUBLIC HOUSE
The Red Lion
South Street. Tel: (0869) 40225
Small pub with cellar and licencee of inverse proportion - take godfather to try the old Armagnacs.
Free House. Licensee: Mr Colin Mead. Opening Hours: 11-3pm 6-11pm. Food Available. Restaurant Specialities: Lobster and game in season. Garden. Recommendations: Good Pub Guide.

STEVENTON
A largely modern village that is dominated by a very large village green, with a causeway which the Benedictine monks built 700 years ago to keep the villagers' feet dry when the stream flooded. The causeway, nearly a mile long, ends in the National Trust priory and the 14th century church; it is still maintained, which is just as well as the stream still floods.
Population: 1,354. Map Ref: E 11.

CHURCH
St Michael

HOTELS
Steventon House Hotel
Milton Hill. OX13 6AB Tel: (0235) 831223
The Timsbury Hotel
High Street. Tel: (0235) 831254

PUBLIC HOUSES
The Cherry Tree Inn
Tel: (0235) 831222
The Fox Inn
Tel: (0235) 831253
The Kings Arms
45 The Green. Tel: (0235) 831639
The North Star Inn
Tel: (0235) 831309
Recommendations: Good Pub Guide.
The Pack Horse Inn
Milton Hill. Tel: (0235) 831231
The Plough
Station Yard. Tel: (0235) 20183

STOKE LYNE
A small farming village with a Norman church and Victorian rectory.
Population: 219. Map Ref: H 4.

CHURCH
St Peter
There is an 800 year old statue of St Peter over the porch.

PUBLIC HOUSE
The Peyton Arms
Tel: (08696) 285

OTHER AMENITIES
TOURS AND SIGHTS
Drivers Companion
Meadow Cottage, The Street. OX6 9SE Tel: (08696) 6733

STONESFIELD
Situated in the Evenlode valley, and famous for its fine quality roofing slates used on the roofs of many Oxford Colleges. There is an attractive early Georgian manor house and a tiny village gaol. A museum has been created to chronicle the history of Stonesfield slate mine.
Population: 1,365. Map Ref: D 6.

CHURCH
St James
An Early English church that underwent a bad restoration in 1876.

PUBLIC HOUSE
The White Horse
Tel: (099389) 604

THE THAMES AT STREATLEY

Brewery: Halls. Licensee: Mr Bishop. Opening Hours: 11am - 2.30pm 6 - 11pm. Food Available: 11.30am - 2pm 6.30 - 10pm. Restaurant Specialities: Carvery. A la Carte. 5 Bedrooms: B&B per person: £13.50. Garden. Children's area.

🐾 🐾 🐾 🐾 🐾 🐾 🐾

STONOR

Stonor valley is one of the most untouched parts of the Chilterns, and Stonor itself is a small flint and brick village consisting of cottages and farms at the entrance to Stonor Park. The deer park is one of the most beautiful in southern England, and Stonor House itself contains a chapel which has been a centre of Catholicism since Tudor times, and a celebrated collection of catholic books and documents in the Library. The house, gardens and park are open to the public during the summer.

Population: 288 (with Pishill). Map Ref: K 12.

PLACES OF INTEREST

Stonor Park

Tel: (049 163) 587

A house and chapel, a centre of Catholicism, set in a secluded wooded dear park in the Chiltern Hills. Built by successive generations of the Stonor family over a period of six generations, since 1190. It is still a family home, but open to the public, with many items of interest on display, including rare furniture, paintings, bronze sculptures and tapestries. There is also a display of model soldiers. *Months Open: April (Sundays only) May - September. Days Open: Sun, Wed and Thurs. Sat in August. Hours Open: 2-5.30pm. Bank Holidays: Bank Holiday Monday 11-5.30pm.*

HOTEL

The Stonor Arms Restaurant and Bar

RG9 6HE Tel: (0491) 63345

18th century Inn set in beautiful countryside.

STRATTON AUDLEY

A pretty stone village with the remains of what once was a Middle Aged castle, built by the Audley family. Stratton Park stands on top of a hill and has wonderful views across the county.

Population: 308. Map Ref: I 5.

CHURCH

St Mary & St Edburga

The church is mainly 14th and 15th century and has late medieval windows.

🐾 🐾 🐾 🐾 🐾 🐾 🐾

STREATLEY-ON-THAMES

Situated on the Berkshire side of the Thames, opposite Goring. This is the Goring Gap, where Ickneild Way (The Ridgeway) crosses the river. The Swan occupies an idyllic riverside site, overlooking the bridge that replaced the original ferry. *Map Ref: H 13.*

HOTEL

The Swan-at-Streatley

RG8 9HR Tel: (0491) 873737

🐾 🐾 🐾 🐾 🐾 🐾 🐾

SUMMERTOWN

A large suburb north of Oxford. *Map Ref: G 8.*

GUEST HOUSE

Lonsdale

312 Banbury Road. Tel: (0865) 54872

RESTAURANTS

Fifteen North Parade

15 North Parade. Tel: (0865) 513773
The Greek Taverna
272 Banbury Road. Tel: (0865) 511472
Specialities: Mezethes. Hours Open: Lunch: 12.00-1.45pm. Dinner: 6.30 - 10.00pm. Last Orders: 10.00pm. Closed Monday lunch and Bank Holidays. Closed Sundays. Lunch: £ 7.50. Credit Cards: Ac. Am. D. V. Seating Capacity: 60. Veg. Parties.
The Lotus House Restaurant
197 Banbury Road. Tel: (0865) 54239
Summertown Coffee House
19 Suffolk House, South Parade. Tel: (0865) 52050

🐾 🐾 🐾 🐾 🐾 🐾 🐾

SUNNINGWELL

A little village of stone houses grouped around a pond. The church has a seven-sided porch which was built in around 1550.
Population: 1,162. Map Ref: F 9.

CHURCH
St Leonard

PUBLIC HOUSE
The Flowing Well Inn
Tel: (0865) 735846

🐾 🐾 🐾 🐾 🐾 🐾 🐾

SUTTON COURTENAY

Half-timbered cottages along winding lanes, and around a spacious green, help make this one of the prettiest villages on the Thames. The Courtenay family owned land here after the Norman Conquest and left their name and an elegant manor house, which is just visible from the main road. There was a royal residence visited by William the Conqueror, and Henry I's first child was born here; the remains form part of the manor. Opposite this house is a building known as the Abbey, but it was actually built by monks from Abingdon in the 14th century. There is a house opposite the church which is one of the oldest houses in Oxfordshire and has been lived in for 800 years. In the churchyard can be found the graves of Lord Asquith, one time Prime Minister, who lived in a house called The Wharf in Sutton Courtenay, and Eric Blair, better known as George Orwell. The church has some Norman details, but is mostly 14th and 15th century and has a late medieval brick porch.
Population: 2,307. Map Ref: F 11.

CHURCH
All Saints

PUBLIC HOUSES
The Fish Inn
Tel: (0235) 848242
The George & Dragon
Church Street. Tel: (0235) 848252
The Swan
The Green. Tel: (0235) 847446

OTHER AMENITIES
GARDEN CENTRE
Richard Mathews Garden Centre
7, Harwell Road. Tel: (0235) 847194

🐾 🐾 🐾 🐾 🐾 🐾 🐾

SWALCLIFFE

A Cotswold ironstone village near the source of the River Avon. The church is part Saxon and part Norman and has a 17th century pulpit and reading desk. Near the church is a medieval tithe barn, still used for farming, which was built by William of Wykeham, founder of New College.
Population: 171. Map Ref: D 2.

CHURCH
St Peter & St Paul

PUBLIC HOUSE
The Stags Head
Tel: (029 578) 232

🐾 🐾 🐾 🐾 🐾 🐾 🐾

SWINBROOK

ST MARY'S, SWINBROOK

SWINBROOK

Situated in the Windrush Valley, Swinbrook is best known for its connections with the Mitford sisters. Nancy Mitford is buried in the churchyard, under a gravestone marked with a mole, the family symbol. There are old stone houses and cottages grouped around the church which stands on a slight rise; it houses the famous Fettiplace monuments; in two separate displays, six generations of the family are carved reclining somewhat uncomfortably in armour. The Fettiplaces were among the greatest landowners in the area and they built a large house in Swinbrook of which no trace now remains. In the 18th century, unfortunately all four brothers died childless, thus the Fettiplaces disappeared from history, leaving just tombs and monuments.
Population: 143. Map Ref: B 7.

CHURCH
St Mary

PUBLIC HOUSE
The Swan Inn
Tel: (099382) 2165
Recommendations: Good Pub Guide.

ﭏ ﭏ ﭏ ﭏ ﭏ ﭏ ﭏ

TACKLEY

Tackley is an unspoiled village, with a large church overlooking the village. Cottages and houses are grouped around the triangular village green. Sir John Harbonne lived here with his 15 children in the Manor House (now demolished) on the green, but the thatched stables and the stone stables of 1616 remain. The probable site of a Roman villa is on the hill across the road from the church and Tackley Park.
Population: 815. Map Ref: F 5.

CHURCH
St Nicholas

PUBLIC HOUSES
The Kings Arms
3 Nethercote Road. Tel: (086983) 334
Sturdys Castle
Tel: (086983) 200

ﭏ ﭏ ﭏ ﭏ ﭏ ﭏ ﭏ

TADMARTON

Derived from the old English 'frog pool', this village is in the valley of the Swale Brook, which flows through the village, eventually becoming the moat at Broughton Castle. The buildings in Main Street are built of the local orange-brown stone.
Map Ref: D 2.

PUBLIC HOUSE
The Lampett Arms
Main Street. Tel: (029578) 260

🐄 🐄 🐄 🐄 🐄 🐄 🐄

TAYNTON
Golden stone thatched cottages nestle on a slope overlooking the River Windrush. Stone was quarried here for Blenheim Palace, St. Paul's Cathedral, Eton College and several Oxford colleges; some 2,000 tons were used in building Windsor castle in 1358-69. It is the most famous of the Oxfordshire limestones.
Population: 73. Map Ref: A 7.

CHURCH
St John Evangelist
This small late-medieval church has an unusual font and carved corbel heads.

🐄 🐄 🐄 🐄 🐄 🐄 🐄

THAME
An historic market town since before the Norman conquest, situated on the River Thame. The town has a wide unspoilt High Street, signifying its importance, with old coaching inns, period houses, shops and restaurants. The houses and shops are very colourful and there are numerous pubs, one of which, The Spread Eagle, was written about by John Fothergill in a book called 'The Diary of an Innkeeper'. There is a Victorian Town Hall, and once a year the Thame Show is held, which is the biggest agricultural event in Oxfordshire. Thame Park, situated south of the town, is a large Georgian house in a huge park; it is built on the site of a Cistercian monastery and there are traces of this in the present building. In 1540, on the Dissolution of the Monasteries, it became the property of Lord Williams of Thame, who was a benefactor of Thame, notably founding a school which is still named after him.
Population: 8,300. Market day: Tuesday. Early closing: Wednesday. Map Ref: J 9.

PLACES OF INTEREST
Rycote Chapel
Ryecote Park. Tel: (08447) 346
An interesting 15th century domestic chapel founded by Richard Quatremayne. The interior is furnished with beautiful Jacobean pews and medieval benches. It is the only remaining part of the Rycote mansion where Sir Henry Norreys entertained Queen Elizabeth I.

Months Open: 15 March - 15 October. Days Open: Daily. Hours Open: Monday-Sat: 9.30am-6.30pm Sunday: 2-6.30pm.

CHURCHES
Congregational Chapel
High Street.
Methodist Chapel
Upper High Street.
St Mary
The church is by the river and the oldest part, built in 1200, is the chancel. As Thame prospered, more aisles were built and the tower heightened. The tomb of Lord Williams and his wife are in the centre of the chancel in front of the altar.

HOTELS
The Black Horse Hotel
11 Cornmarket. Tel: (084 421) 2886
A small, family-run hotel offering good food , well-stocked bars and hospitality.
BEDROOMS: 6 Single, (6 en suite, 6 TV, 6 phone, 6 tea/coffee) B&B £ 22.00 - £ 24.00. 3 Double, (3 en suite, 3 TV, 3 phone, 3 tea/coffee) B&B £ 33.00 - £ 35.00. 1 Twin, (1 TV, 1 tea/coffee) B&B £ 34.00 - £ 36.00. RESTAURANT: Traditional Cuisine. Lunch: £ 5.00. Dinner: £ 11.00. HOTEL INFORMATION: CF. W. B. F. 17 space Car Park. Dogs. Credit Cards: AC.
Weekend Breaks: 2 nights: £ 45.00. 3 nights: £ 67.50. Allowance towards dinner: £ 10.00.
Essex House
149 Chinnor Road. OX9 3LS Tel: (084 421) 7567
The Four Horseshoes
Park Street. OX9 Tel: (084 421) 2029
The Spread Eagle Hotel
Corn Market. OX9 2BW Tel: (084 421) 3661
Converted 17th century coaching Inn.
Thatcher's Hotel
29-30 Lower High Street. Tel: (084 421) 6532
The Wellington Hotel
Wellington Street. OX9 3BW Tel: (084 421) 2682

RESTAURANTS
The Drunken Chef Restaurant
1 Buttermarket Lane. Tel: (084 421) 4824
Friends
8 Swan Walk. Tel: (084 421) 5152
Greys Brasserie
21 Cornmarket. Tel: (084 421) 6626
Mallards Wine Bar & Restaurant
87 High Street. Tel: (084 421) 6679
The Pizza Box
86 High Street. Tel: (084 421) 6266
The Prince of India Tandoori Restaurant
7 Upper High Street. Tel: (084 421) 6690
Ridges Eating House
19 High Street. Tel: (084 421) 2175
The Swan Restaurant/Freehouse/Hotel

9 Upper High Street. Tel: (084 421) 7207
Specialities: From game and seafood to lasagne. Hours Open: Lunch: 12 - 2.30. Tea: Afternoons. Dinner: 7.00 +. Last Orders: 10.30. Lunch: £ 7.50. Tea: £ 0.70. Dinner: £ 12.50. House Wine: £ 5.15. Credit Card: V. Seating Capacity: 34. Vegetarian. Banquets. Parties. Weddings. Recommendations: ER.M.

Thatchers
29/30 Lower High Street. OX9 2AA
Tel: (084 421) 3058/2146

PUBLIC HOUSES

The Abingdon Arms
High Street. Tel: (084421) 2969
The Bird Cage Inn
4 Cornmarket. Tel: (084421) 2046
The Cross Keys
Park Street. Tel: (084421) 2147
The Falcon
Thame Park Road. Tel: (084421) 2118
The Fox
High Street. Tel: (084421) 5803
The Nags Head
High Street. Tel: (084421) 2028
The Oxford Arms
Tel: (084421) 2933
The Rising Sun
Easington Terrace. Tel: (084421) 4206
The Saracens Head
The Buttermarket. Tel: (084421) 2931
The Six Bells
High Street. Tel: (084421) 2088
The Star & Garter
Wellington Street. Tel: (084421) 2166
The Two Brewers
North Street. Tel: (084421) 2381

OTHER AMENITIES

HOSPITAL
Thame Community Hospital
East Street. Tel: (084421) 2727
LEISURE CENTRE
Thame Sports and Arts Centre
Oxford Road. Tel: (084421) 5607
SNOOKER CENTRE
Thame Snooker Club
Chesnut Yard. Tel: (084421) 7166
SPORTS CLUBS
Chinnor Rugby Football Club
Towersey Playing Fields. Tel: (084421) 3735
Thame Sports Club
Queens Road. Tel: (084421) 2401
Thame United F C
Windmill Road. Tel: (084421) 3017
THEATRE

Players Theatre
Nelson Street. Tel: (084421) 2012
TOURIST OFFICE
Tourist Information Centre
Town Hall, High Street. Tel: (084421) 2834

❧ ❧ ❧ ❧ ❧ ❧ ❧

THE BARTONS

The Bartons consists of three villages rolled into one, with the picturesque River Dorn running between them all. Westcote Barton has a charming church in the Perpendicular style, which is painted with the vivid colours distinctive to the Medieval Age. Middle Barton consists of old stone houses on either side of a ford stretching across the Dorn. Steeple Barton consists of a farm, cottages and a large church. The church has a 15th century tower and although the interior is mostly plain, there are some very interesting stone carvings. Looking across a lake from the churchyard, you can see Barton Abbey, which is an ivy-covered house situated on a site of what used to be the cell of Osney Abbey before the Dissolution of the Monasteries. *Population: 1,798. Map Ref: E 5.*

❧ ❧ ❧ ❧ ❧ ❧ ❧

THRUPP

This canalside hamlet was once the home of people working on the barges of the Oxford Canal, mainly transporting coal from the Midlands to Oxford. Now the wharf and basin are used to service the pleasure side of canal activities.
Map Ref: F 6.

PUBLIC HOUSE

The Boat Inn
Thrupp. Tel: (08675) 4279

❧ ❧ ❧ ❧ ❧ ❧ ❧

TOWERSEY

Originally in Buckinghamshire, Towersy was 'transferred' to Oxfordshire in 1939. It has a village pond, farms and a 14th century church.
Population: 435. Map Ref: K 9.

PUBLIC HOUSE

The Three Horseshoes
Tel: (084421) 2322
Recommendations: Good Pub Guide.

OTHER AMENITIES

GARDEN CENTRE
Lashlake Nurseries
Chinnor Road. Tel: (084421) 2392

🐦 🐦 🐦 🐦 🐦 🐦 🐦

UFFINGTON
A large chalk and brick village in the Vale of the White Horse. Much of the chalk comes from local chalk pits. Some cottages are thatched. Feast day was an ancient ritual in this part of the world, where much eating and drinking took place; there were also two popular local sports, wrestling and backswording (fencing with cudgels) held on a platform in the churchyard. Elsewhere there were stalls and peep shows.
Population: 719. Map Ref: B 11.

PLACES OF INTEREST
The Vale of the White Horse
An Iron Age white horse is carved into the hillside, the only prehistoric white horse of the many in the land, close to the ancient hill fort of Uffington Castle. Its origin is shrouded in mystery, but in many versions it was carved to commemorate Alfred's victory over the Danes at Ashdown in 871. It is 370 feet long and 130 feet high. It has been suggested that it is moving up the hillside. Below it is Dragon Hill, where St George was supposed to have slain his dragon.
Tom Brown School Museum
Broad Street.
Tel: (036782) 675
Museum of the life and works of Thomas Hughes, who spent much of his youth in Uffington, with special reference to Tom Brown, his most famous work.
Months Open: Easter-September. Days Open: Weekends. Hours Open: 2-5pm. Bank Holidays: Open Bank Holiday 2-5pm Closed on the late summer B H Weekend.

CHURCHES

THE WHITE HORSE, UFFINGTON

Friends Meeting House
St Mary
There is a large 13th century church known as the Cathedral of the Vale, with an octagonal tower which lost its spire in a storm.

PUBLIC HOUSES
The Fox & Hounds
Tel: (036782) 680
The White Horse
Woolstone. Tel: (036782) 566

🐦 🐦 🐦 🐦 🐦 🐦 🐦

UPPER BASILDON
Map Ref: H 14.

PUBLIC HOUSE
The Red Lion
Aldworth Road. Tel: (0491) 671234
Licensee: Mr J A Sessions.

🐦 🐦 🐦 🐦 🐦 🐦 🐦

UPPER HEYFORD
A pretty village with stone streets leading down to the Oxford canal. There is huge stone tithe barn built for William of Wykeham in the 14th century which is still owned by New College Oxford, which he founded. There is a large air base here.
Population: 2,355. Map Ref: F 5.

CHURCHES
Christ Tabernacle Community Church
Tel: (086982) 2544
St Mary

PUBLIC HOUSE
The Three Horseshoes
Tel: (086982) 2700

🐦 🐦 🐦 🐦 🐦 🐦 🐦

UPPER LAMBOURN
Map Ref: B 13.

PUBLIC HOUSE
The Malt Shovel
Tel: (0488) 71623

🐦 🐦 🐦 🐦 🐦 🐦 🐦

UPPER WARDINGTON
Map Ref: F 1.
PLACES OF INTEREST

High Wardington House
Tel: (0295) 750750

HOTEL
The Plough
OX17 7SP Tel: (0295) 750476

PUBLIC HOUSE
The Red Lion
Tel: (0295) 750288

🍂 🍂 🍂 🍂 🍂 🍂 🍂

WALLINGFORD
Wallingford received its first charter in 1155, making it one of the oldest boroughs in the country. A 900 foot bridge stands on the site of an ancient ford, giving access to this charming riverside town. Wallingford is a crucial crossing point of the Thames, and as such is of great stategic importance. William the Conqueror crossed the river here in 1067; there are remains of a Norman castle which was noted for the strength of its defences, tested for the last time when it was the last Royalist stronghold to surrender. There is a 17th century Town Hall, many timber framed buildings, lovely streets, houses and inns and a beautiful view over the bridge. The church in the market square has an impressive tower.
Population: 6,229. Market day: Thursday. Early closing: Wednesday. Map Ref: H 12.

PLACES OF INTEREST
Wallingford Castle
Castle Street.
Months Open: March-October . Days Open: Daily. Hours Open: 10am-6pm.
Wallingford Museum
Flint House, High Street.
Tel: (0491) 35065
Local history museum in a 16th century flint house showing 1000 years of the town's history, including a display on Wallingford Castle.
Months Open: All Year. Days Open: Tuesday - Saturday Sunday during June-August. Hours Open: Tues-Fri: 2-5pm Saturday 10.30am-12.30pm, 2-5pm Sunday 2-5pm. Bank Holidays: B H Monday 2-5pm.

HOTELS
The George Hotel
High Street. OX10 0BS Tel: (0491) 36665
Old world charm, with modern facilities.
BEDROOMS: 14 Single, (14 en suite, 14 TV, 14 phone, 14 tea/

coffee) B&B £ 49.50 - £ 53.50. 23 Double, (23 en suite, 23 TV, 23 phone, 23 tea/coffee) B&B £ 67.00 1 Twin, (1 en suite, 1 phone, 1 tea/coffee) RESTAURANT: French/English Cuisine. Lunch: £ 13.50. Dinner: £ 14.50. House Wine: £ 7.25. À La Carte: £ 15.00. HOTEL INFORMATION: C. W. B. F. 55 space Car Park. Dogs. N/S 400 years old. Credit Cards: AC. AM. D. V. Recommendations: AA***. ER 66%. M. RAC ***.
Weekend Breaks: 2 nights: £ 70.00. 3 nights: £ 105.00. Allowance towards dinner: £ 14.50.
Springs Hotel
North Stoke. OX9 6BE Tel: (0491) 36687
Elegant country house hotel overlooking lake and gardens

GUEST HOUSE
The Nook
Thames Street. Tel: (0491) 34214

RESTAURANTS
The Prince of India
31 High Street. Tel: (0491) 35394
Stoneys Restaurant
4 High Street. Tel: (0491) 36249
Specialities: Seafood and steaks in wine sauces. Hours Open: Dinner: 7.30pm. Last Orders: 10.30pm. Credit Cards: AC. V. Seating Capacity: 36. Veg. Parties.
Upstairs & Downstairs
28 High Street. Tel: (0491) 34078

PUBLIC HOUSES
The Coach & Horses
12 Kinecroft. Tel: (0491) 25054
Village green family pub.
Brewery: Fullers. Licensee: Mr & Mrs Humphries. Food Available: 12 - 2.30pm 7 - 10pm. Garden. Childrens area.
The Coachmakers Arms
St Marys Street. Tel: (0491) 39382
The Dolphin
St Marys Street. Tel: (0491) 37377
The Green Tree
St Leonards Square. Tel: (0491) 35355
The Kings Head
St Martins Street. Tel: (0491) 38309
Little House Round The Corner By The Brook
St Leonards Lane. Tel: (0491) 37037
The Norman Knight
Wantage Road. Tel: (0491) 35218
The Plough Inn
St Johns Road. Tel: (0491) 35400
The Town Arms
Reading Road. Tel: (0491) 35411

TEA ROOMS
Annies Tea Rooms
79 High Street. Tel: (0491) 36308

Cobblers
2 The Arcade. Tel: (0491) 33698
Lamb Coffee Shop
Lamb Arcade High Street. Tel: (0491) 33581
Valentines Cafe
66 High Street. Tel: (0491) 34522

OTHER AMENITIES

CAR HIRE
Lamb Garage
Castle Street. Tel: (0491) 36149
CAR HIRE/SELF DRIVE
Peugeot Talbot Rental
Jim Pink (Wallingford) Ltd, Wood Street.
Tel: (0491) 36017
Thames Valley Rental
Total Garage, High Street. Tel: (0491) 37596
STORE
Petits of Wallingford
46, St Mary's Street. Tel: (0491) 35253
HOSPITAL
Wallingford Community Hospital
Reading Road. Tel: (0491) 25533
SAUNA
Thames Sauna
21A, St Marys Street. Tel: (0491) 37124
SPORTS CLUB
Wallingford Sports Trust
Hithercroft Road. Tel: (0491) 35044
THEATRE
Sinodun Players Dramatic Society
The Corn Exchange, Market Place. Tel: (0491) 39336
WINE BAR
The Wine Bar
85, High Street. Tel: (0491) 33426

WANTAGE

Situated on the Roman Portway below the downs, this old market town seems to be of Saxon origin. Situated in the Vale of the White Horse, Wantage was the birthplace in 849 of King Alfred, whose statue stands in the market square. There are a number of period houses, mainly made of red and local blue-glazed bricks. Wantage prospered in the Middle Ages and became the centre for the western end of the Vale of White Horse.

Population: 8,741. Market day: Wednesday/ Saturday. Early closing: Thursday. Map Ref: D 12.

PLACES OF INTEREST

Vale and Downland Museum Centre
The Old Surgery, Church Street.
Tel: (02357) 66838
An attractive museum telling the story of Wantage and the Vale of the White Horse over the years. Situated in the picturesque Church Street.
Months Open: All Year. Days Open: Daily except for Mondays Hours Open: Tues-Sat: 10.30am - 4.30pm. Sunday: 2-5pm. Bank Holidays: Open some B H Mondays.

CHURCHES
Methodist Chapel
Newbury Street.
St Peter & St Paul

HOTELS

The Bear Hotel
Market Place. OX12 8AB Tel: (023 57) 66366
16th C. Coaching Inn in centre of historic market town.
The Bell Inn
Market Square. Tel: (023 57) 3718
The Blue Boar Hotel
Newbury Street. OX12 8BS Tel: (023 57) 3209

RESTAURANTS

The Ayesha Tandoori Restaurant
2 - 4 Mill Street. Tel: (023 57) 4874
Indian Cuisine. Specialities: Massala, Moglai, Pasanda, Thali dishes, Korai, Bhuna and Tandoori dishes. Hours Open: Lunch: 12 - 2.30pm. Dinner: 6-12.00pm. Last Orders: 11.30pm. Closed Christmas Day. Open Sundays. Dinner: £ 10.50. House Wine: £ 4.95. Credit Cards: AC. AM. D. V. Seating Capacity: 80. Veg. Banquets. Parties. Weddings.
Beetons Restaurant
The Post Office Vaults, Market Square. Tel: (023 57) 69901
The Peking Dynasty
Newbury Street. Tel: (023 57) 2517
Pizza Capri
8 Regent Shopping, Mall Newbury Street.
Tel: (023 57) 66625
The Villa Chinese Restaurant
3 Mill Street. Tel: (023 57) 68281

PUBLIC HOUSES

The Abingdon Arms
Grove Street. Tel: (02357) 3957
The Bay Tree
Grove. Tel: (02357) 3494
The Bell Inn
Market Place. Tel: (02357) 3718
18th century country inn with good food. Traditional beer and a friendly atmosphere.
Brewery: Morlands. Licensee: Ms Susan Ann Stanton. Opening Hours: 10.30am - 11 pm. Food Available: 12 - 2pm. 3 Bedrooms: B&B per person: £15.

The Shears
39 Mill Street. Tel: (02357) 2650
The Shoulder of Mutton
Wallingford Street. Tel: (02357) 2835
The Vaults Wine Bar
Old Post Office Vaults, Market Place. Tel: (02357) 67223
The Wheatsheaf Inn
28 Grove Street. Tel: (02357) 4622

TEA ROOMS
The Green Ginger Tea Room
Tel:

OTHER AMENITIES
CINEMA
Regent Cinema
2, Newbury Street. Tel: (02357) 67878
GARDEN CENTRE
Kingstone Lisle Nurseries
Kingstone Lisle Park. Tel: (036782) 216
LEISURE CENTRES
Recreation Ground
Manor Road. Tel: (02357) 69895
Wantage Recreation Centre
Portway. Tel: (02357) 66201
SPORTS CLUB
Wantage Town Football Club
Manor Road. Tel: (02357) 4781

🐾 🐾 🐾 🐾 🐾 🐾 🐾

WARBOROUGH
A village with a large green with cottages and houses of mixed periods. The name 'Warborough' is derived from the Old English, which roughly translated means 'watch hill', referring to Town Hill, the hill behind the town, which provides a natural look-out.
Population: 985. Map Ref: H 11.

CHURCH
St Laurence
Mainly Early English, this church has a three stage tower built in 1666.

PUBLIC HOUSES
Nellys
The Green. Tel: (086732) 8761
The Six Bells
The Green South. Tel: (086732) 8265

🐾 🐾 🐾 🐾 🐾 🐾 🐾

WARDINGTON

A village with orange-brown ironstone farms and houses with wide grass verges. There is a small Jacobean manor house visible through impressive wrought iron gates.
Population: 531. Map Ref: F 1.

CHURCHES
St Mary Magdalen
Wesleyan Chapel

OTHER AMENITIES
BOAT HIRE
Holiday Charente
Old Bonhams. Tel: (0295) 758282

🐾 🐾 🐾 🐾 🐾 🐾 🐾

WATERPERRY
A peaceful village near the river Thame, well known for its nursery. Waterperry House has a 17th century east wing and was added to in the 18th and 19th centuries.
Population: 144. Map Ref: H 8.

PLACES OF INTEREST
Waterperry Gardens
Tel: (08447) 254
Each year in the 83 acres of gardens, there is a week-long tented exhibition called 'Art in Action' where craftsmen exhibit their skills and sell their wares.
Months Open: All Year. Days Open: Daily. Hours Open: Mon-Fri: 10am-5.30pm (winter 10am-4.30pm) Weekends: 10am-6pm (winter 10am-4.30pm) .

🐾 🐾 🐾 🐾 🐾 🐾 🐾

WATLINGTON
Watlington stands astride the prehistoric Icknield Way, which stretched from Wiltshire to the Wash. It has a 17th century Town Hall built by Thomas Stonor in 1664 which was also used as a grammar school and a covered market; there are narrow windy streets and many half-timbered houses. Watlington used to have a wide array of inns, but a 19th century Methodist bought six and closed them all down. In the Domesday Book there were five mills listed and the land was owned by the D'Oilly barons and Preaux Abbey. Later a castle was built, of which there are no remains.
Population: 2,159. Map Ref: J 11.

HOTELS
The Hare & Hounds
Crouching Street.   Tel: (049 161) 2329

The Well House Restaurant and Hotel
34-40 High Street. OX5 9PY Tel: (049 161) 3333
The Well House is a small family-run restaurant with rooms, in the centre of the village.
BEDROOMS: 1 Single, (1 en suite, 1 TV, 1 phone, 1 tea/coffee) 3 Double, (3 en suite, 3 TV, 3 phone, 3 tea/coffee) B&B £ 47.50 - £ 53.50. 4 Twin, (4 en suite, 4 TV, 4 phone, 4 tea/coffee) B&B £ 47.50 - £ 53.50. RESTAURANT: International Cuisine. Lunch: £ 13.50. Dinner: £ 13.50. House Wine: £ 6.00. À La Carte:£22.00. HOTEL INFORMATION: CF. W. B. F. 15 space Car Park: Credit Cards: AC. AM. D. V.
Weekend Breaks: 2 nights: £ 70.00. 3 nights: £ 105.00. Allowance towards dinner: £ 13.50.

PUBLIC HOUSES
The Carriers Arms
Hills Road. Tel: (049161) 3470
Chequers
Love Lane.
Recommendations: Good Pub Guide.
The Fox & Hounds
Shirburn Street. Tel: (049161) 2142

OTHER AMENITIES
BUS & COACH SERVICES
House's Watlington Buses
Brook Street. Tel: (049 161) 2319
HOSPITAL
Watlington & District Hospital
Hill Road. Tel: (049 161) 2235

🐾 🐾 🐾 🐾 🐾 🐾 🐾

WENDLEBURY
Wendlebury is a pleasant mixture of old and new houses with a stream running down the side of the street. There is an 18th century manor house.
Population: 531. Map Ref: H 6.

CHURCH
St Giles

PUBLIC HOUSE
The Red Lion
Tel: (0869) 252514

🐾 🐾 🐾 🐾 🐾 🐾 🐾

WEST HAGBOURNE
A small village, twinned with East Hagbourne, which has a combination of new houses mixed in with old farms and cottages.
Population: 315. Map Ref: F 12.

PUBLIC HOUSE
The Horse & Harrow
Main Street. Tel: (0235) 850223

🐾 🐾 🐾 🐾 🐾 🐾 🐾

WEST HANNEY
An old village in the Vale of the White Horse which has an early Georgian house in the centre.
Population: 488. Map Ref: D 11.

CHURCH
St James
This large church had a tower that collapsed in 1946.

PUBLIC HOUSES
The Lamb Inn
School Road. Tel: (023587) 540
The Plough Inn
Tel: (023587) 674

🐾 🐾 🐾 🐾 🐾 🐾 🐾

WEST HENDRED
A small attractive village that has a 14th century church by the brook. There are lovely walks in this area crossing Grimms Ditch to the Ridgeway on to the Downs.
Population: 334. Map Ref: E 11.

CHURCH
Holy Trinity

PUBLIC HOUSE
The Hare Inn
OX12 8RH Tel: (0235) 833249

🐾 🐾 🐾 🐾 🐾 🐾 🐾

WEST ILSLEY
Nestled up against the Berkshire Downs, West Ilsey is a small quiet village with a Victorian church. There are tracks leading up to the Ridgeway.
Map Ref: E 13.

CHURCH
All Saints

HOTEL
The Harrow
RG16 0AR Tel: (063 528) 260

🐾 🐾 🐾 🐾 🐾 🐾 🐾

WESTON-ON-THE-GREEN

Centred around the green from which the village takes its name, the older and prettier part of the village is down a side road leading to Bletchingdon. Until the heir was killed in the First World War, the Bertie family owned the manor here and completely rebuilt the church in 1743 after it was burnt down.

Population: 473. Early closing: Saturday. Map Ref: G 6.

CHURCH
St Mary

The iron cross by the pulpit comes from the masthead of a ship in the Spanish Armada.

HOTEL
Weston Manor Hotel

OX6 8QL Tel: (0869) 50621

Magnificent country house hotel, with log fires.

RESTAURANT
Little Chef

Weston Garage. Tel: (0869) 50484

PUBLIC HOUSES
The Ben Johnson

Tel: (0869) 50320

Chequers Inn

Tel: (0869) 50319

OTHER AMENITIES
SPORTS CLUB
Oxford Gliding Club

Tel: (086989) 265

🌿 🌿 🌿 🌿 🌿 🌿 🌿

WHEATLEY

Developed between Roman and Victorian times, many buildings apart from the church were designed by G E Street. The High Street has some stone houses, including a manor, and there are two farms in Crown Road which are 17th century. There is a village lock-up which is a pyramid with a ball on the top.

Population: 3,506. Map Ref: H 8.

CHURCHES
Congregational Chapel
St Mary

GE Street-designed

RESTAURANTS
The Harvester Restaurant

Oxford Road. Tel: (086 77) 5270

The White Hart

High Street. Tel: (086 77) 4624

PUBLIC HOUSES
The Kings Arms

Church Road. Tel: (08677) 2921

The Plough Inn

London Road. Tel: (08677) 2949

The Sun Inn

Tel: (08677) 2264

OTHER AMENITIES
GARDEN CENTRES
Cramphorn plc

London Road. Tel: (08677) 3057

Waterperry Gardens & Nurseries

Nr Wheatley. Tel: (08447) 226

🌿 🌿 🌿 🌿 🌿 🌿 🌿

WHITCHURCH

This pretty village on the Thames is backed by typical Chiltern woodland. It has a mixture of brick and flint cottages, Georgian and Edwardian villas. Crossing the Victorian iron tollbridge to Pangbourne costs 4p.

Population: 832. Map Ref: H 14.

CHURCH
St Mary

A VIEW OF THE MILL & ST MARY'S, WHITCHURCH

113

ST MARY'S, WITNEY

PUBLIC HOUSES

The Ferryboat Inn
High Street. Tel: (07357) 2161
The Greyhound
High Street. Tel: (07357) 2160

🔔 🔔 🔔 🔔 🔔 🔔 🔔

WHITCHURCH HILL

A small settlement that stands at the top of the hill, Whitchurch proper is at the bottom of the hill.

CHURCH
St John Baptist

PUBLIC HOUSE
The Sun
Hill Bottom. Tel: (07357) 2260

OTHER AMENITIES
HOLIDAY ACCOMODATION
Starveall Farm
90, Wootton Road. Tel: (0235) 32719

🔔 🔔 🔔 🔔 🔔 🔔 🔔

WIGGINTON

Situated 400 feet up a hillside, there are some Roman remains south of the village, and also some old stone houses and a church.
Population: 199. Map Ref: D 3.

CHURCH
St Giles

OTHER AMENITIES

GOLF CLUB
Tadmarton Heath GC
Tel: (0608) 73004

🔔 🔔 🔔 🔔 🔔 🔔 🔔

WITNEY

The earliest mill in this world-famous blanket-making town, mentioned in the Domesday Book, was recorded in 1277, but it was in the 18th and 19th century that the industry reached its peak, when there were 150 looms in the town, employing 3,000 people. 'Earlys' of Witney are still making blankets, and it is said that the water of the river Windrush has particular qualities that contribute to the softness of the blankets. Church Green is dominated by the 156 foot spire of the 13th century church of St Mary, a landmark for miles around, to which more aisles and chapels were added as Witney grew more prosperous. At Mount House was discovered the 12th century remains of the Bishop of Winchester's palace. The Market Square has several notable buildings, including a medieval meeting place in the Buttercross, the 17th century pillared Town Hall, the Corn Exchange, and old coaching inns. The old Blanket Hall of 1720 has a curious one-handed clock.
Population: 14,215. Map Ref: C 7.

PLACES OF INTEREST
Cogges Manor Farm - Farm Museum.
Tel: (0993) 72602
A 13th century manor house, and Edwardian farmhouse

are part of this 19 acre museum, showing traditional farming skills of yesteryear. Regular demonstrations of blacksmithing, hurdle making, sheep shearing, butter churning, and hand milking. Livestock typical of the period of the turn of the century can be seen. There is a Visitor centre and a cafeteria.

Months Open: 29 March - 6 November. Days Open: Tuesday - Sunday. Hours Open: 10.30am - 5.30pm .10.30am - 4.30pm in Oct & Nov. Bank Holiday Mondays 10.30am - 5.30pm.

CHURCHES

Friends Meeting House
Wood Green.
Holy Trinity
Wood Green.
Methodist Chapel
High Street.
St Hugh (RC)
St Mary

HOTELS
The Court Inn
43 Bridge Street. OX8 6DA Tel: (0993) 3228
Large Inn with simple comfortable rooms.
The Fleece Hotel
11 Church Green. OX8 6AZ Tel: (0993) 702263
The Greystones Lodge Hotel
34 Tower Hill. OX8 5ES Tel: (0993) 771898
Standing in its own grounds. 1 mile Witney centre.
The House of Windsor
31 West End. Tel: (0993) 704277
The Marlborough Hotel
28 Market Square. OX8 7BB Tel: (0993) 776353
Centrally located. Ideal touring Cotswolds, Oxford.
The Red Lion Hotel
Corn Street. Tel: (0993) 703149

RESTAURANTS
The Capital Restaurant
152 Corn Street. Tel: (0993) 703285
The House of Windsor
31 West End. Tel: (0993) 704277
Shapla Indian Cuisine
74 High Street. Tel: (0993) 703430

PUBLIC HOUSES
The Butchers Arms
104 Corn Street. Tel: (0993) 705747
The Carpenters Arms
132 Newland. Tel: (0993) 702206
Chequers Inn
47 Corn Street. Tel: (0993) 702492
The Eagle Vaults
18 The Hill High Street. Tel: (0993) 703503

The Elm Tree
21 West End. Tel: (0993) 702311
The Holly Bush Inn
35 Corn Street. Tel: (0993) 702438
The New Inn
Corn Street. Tel: (0993) 703807
The Plough Inn
High Street. Tel: (0993) 704430
The Robin Hood Inn
Hailey Road. Tel: (0993) 702538
The Rowing Machine
Windrush Valley Road. Tel: (0993) 703386
The Three Horseshoes
78 Corn Street. Tel: (0993) 703086
The Three Pigeons Inn
Wood Green. Tel: (0993) 702803
The Windrush Inn
Burford Road. Tel: (0993) 702612

OTHER AMENITIES
ART GALLERY
Tuppence Coloured
8, West End. Tel: (0993) 772777
GARDEN CENTRES
Dovecote
53, High Street. Tel: (0993) 702537
Great Mills
Thorney Leys Park, Ducklington Lane. Tel: (0993) 78981
HEALTH CLUBS
Jazzercise
65, Oxford Hill. Tel: (0993) 772892
Palace Fitness Studio
29/31, Market Square. OX8 6AW Tel: (0993) 702494
Gymnasium/Fitness Studio
Months Open: All year. Days Open: All week. Hours Open: 10 am - 10 pm Weekends 10 am - 3 pm. Open Bank Holidays. Expert tuition on fitness/toning/circuit training; Rehabilitation/weight loss and weight gain, weight training; Supervised sessions; Sauna; Solarium; Bar and television rest area; Personal programmes written out for individuals. Rates: Full single : cash

THE BRIDGE, WITNEY

for year, £175: Joint; £285. Proprietor: Mr Alan Winterbourne.

HOSPITAL

Witney Community Hospital

Witney. Tel: (0993) 771211

LEISURE CENTRE

Windrush Sports Centre

Witan Way. Tel: (0993) 778444

NIGHT CLUB

Palace

31, Market Square. Tel: (0993) 778100

SPORTS CLUBS

Bee's Pool Club

64, Corn Street. Tel: (0993) 703385

Witney Town Football Club

Marriotts Close. Tel: (0993) 702549

TOURIST OFFICE

Tourist Information Centre

Town Hall, Market Square. Tel: (0993) 4379

TOURS AND SIGHTS

South Midland

Windrush Court, 56a High Street. Tel: (0993) 76679

🐾 🐾 🐾 🐾 🐾 🐾 🐾

WOLVERCOTE

At its lower end, Wolvercote becomes a riverside village with the remains of a former Benedictine house called Godstow nunnery. King Stephen visited the nunnery on its dedication in 1138 and it was a Royalist stronghold in the Civil War until it was burnt down by the Parliamentarians in 1645. Fair Rosamund Clifford is closely associated with the nunnery, where, having fled there after Queen Eleanor discovered about her affair with Henry II, she is meant to have died of a broken heart.

Population: 5,963. Map Ref: F 8.

CHURCHES

Baptist Chapel

Godstow Road.

St Peter

PUBLIC HOUSES

The Plough Inn

Tel: (0865) 56969

The Red Lion

Godstow Road. Tel: (0865) 52722

The Trout Inn

196 Godstow Road. Tel: (0865) 54485

OTHER AMENITIES

CAR HIRE/SELF DRIVE

Kenning

Oxford Travel Lodge,Woodstock Road.Tel:(0865) 511232

WOODCOTE

Map Ref: I 13.

HOTEL

The Chilton Chase Lodge Hotel

Goring Road. Tel: (0491) 680775

OTHER AMENITIES

GARDEN CENTRE

Ashby & Son

Reading Road. Tel: (0491) 680335

🐾 🐾 🐾 🐾 🐾 🐾 🐾

WOODSTOCK

Since early times Kings of England have enjoyed hunting in the Forest of Wychwood, and after Henry I built a hunting lodge at Woodstock, the town grew up outside its gates, inhabited by those he evicted by enclosing their land as a hunting reserve. The town's prosperity was based on its fairs and markets, on bell-casting and glove-making, which still exists. No mention can be made of Woodstock without mention of Blenheim Palace, the magnificent 18th century home of the Duke of Marlborough, and the birth place of Sir Winston Churchill. There is an interesting museum, in the 16th century Fletchers House, which contains a permanent exhibition on the county's development. Outside is a set of stocks with five leg holes. The town is visited by thousands of people from far and wide, and with its fine buildings, renowned inns, antique and gift shops, presents a prosperous image to the world.

Population: 3,158. Early closing: Wednesday. Map Ref: E 6.

PLACES OF INTEREST

Blenheim Palace (picture opposite page)

Tel: (0993) 811325

Birthplace of Winston Churchill in 1874, designed by Sir John Vanburgh (after plans by Wren had been rejected) with gardens laid out by 'Capability' Brown and built of golden stone from the Taynton quarries. Presented by Queen Anne on behalf of 'a grateful nation' to John Churchill, First Duke of Marlborough, after his military success over the French at the Battle of Blenheim in 1704. One of the most spectacular buildings in Europe, the house alone covers seven acres, and the grounds a further 2,500 acres. It contains a fine collection of furniture, paintings and tapestries, plus an exhibition of Churchilliana. There is a butterfly house, restaurant , an adventure playground. *Months Open: Park: All Year. Palace: Mid-March - October. Days Open: Park: Daily. Palace: Daily.Hours Open: Park: 9am-5pm. Palace: 10.30am -6pm (last admission 5pm).*

Oxfordshire County Museum

Fletcher's House, Park Street.

Tel: (0993) 811456

Shows the history of the whole county, with temporary exhibitions on a variety of themes.

Months Open: All Year. Days Open: Daily. Hours Open: Monday-Friday: 10am-5pm. Saturday :10am-6pm. Sunday 2-6pm. Bank Holidays: Closed Good Friday.

CHURCHES

Chapel of St Andrew
Methodist Chapel

Oxford Road.

St Hugh (RC)
St Mary Magdalene
Union Chapel

Hensington Road.

HOTELS

The Bear

Park Street. OX7 1SZ Tel: (0993) 811511

Ancient coaching inn which has been converted to a luxury hotel. The interior offers exceptional character and a first class restaurant.

*BEDROOMS: 5 Single, (5 en suite, 5 TV, 5 phone, 5 tea/coffee) B&B £58.00 - £74.00. 13 Double, (13 en suite, 13 TV, 13 phone, 13 tea/coffee) B&B £111.00 - £136.00. 19 Twin, (19 en suite, 19 TV, 19 phone, 19 tea/coffee) B&B £111.00 - £136.00. 1 Family, (1 en suite, 1 TV, 1 phone, 1 tea/coffee) £111.00 - £136.00. 3 Four Posters, 3 Suites. RESTAURANT: Traditional Cuisine. Lunch: £14.60. Tea: £2.95. Dinner: £16.95. House Wine: £8.35. À La Carte: £20.00. Specialities: Local Game. HOTEL INFORMATION: CF. W. B. F. 40 space Car Park. Dogs. Credit Cards: AC. AM. D. V. Recommendations: AA ***. ER. M. RAC. Weekend Breaks: 2 nights: £116.00. 3 nights: £174.00. Allowance towards dinner: £16.95.*

The Feathers Hotel

Market Street . OX7 1SX Tel: (0993) 812291

The Feathers is a privately owned 17th century hotel furnished with antiques, chintzes, fresh flowers, books and log fires.

*BEDROOMS: 1 Single, (1 en suite, 1 TV, 1 phone) B&B £50.00 - £60.00. 6 Double, (6 en suite, 6 TV, 6 phone) B&B £72.00 - £105.00. 5 Twin, (5 en suite, 5 TV, 5 phone) B&B £72.00 - £105.00. 3 Family, (3 en suite, 3 TV, 3 phone) £72.00 - £105.00. RESTAURANT: English/French Cuisine. Lunch: £12.50. Dinner: £18.50. House Wine: £8.50. À La Carte: £20.00. HOTEL INFORMATION: CF. Credit Cards: AC. AM. D. V. Recommendations: AA **. ER. M.*

The Kings Arms Hotel/ Wheelers Restaurant

Market Street. OX7 1ST Tel: (0993) 811412

16th C. Inn on main Oxford-Stratford Road

BEDROOMS: 2 Single, (2 en suite, 2 TV, 2 phone, 2 tea/coffee,) 4 Double, (4 en suite, 4 TV, 4 phone, 4 tea/coffee,) 3 Twin, (3 en

*suite, 3 TV, 3 phone, 3 tea/coffee,) RESTAURANT: Fish Restaurant Lunch: £9.95. Dinner: £15.50. House Wine: £6.95. Credit Cards: AC. AM. D. V. Recommendations: AA **. Weekend Breaks: 2 nights: £30.00. 3 nights: £30.00. Allowance towards dinner: £15.50.*

The Marlborough Arms

Oxford Street. OX7 1TS Tel: (0993) 811227

15th C. Coaching Inn close to Blenheim Palace

The Punchbowl Inn

12 Oxford Street. Tel: (0993) 811218

The Star Inn

22 Market Place. Tel: (0993) 811373

Vickers Hotel

7 Market Place. Tel: (0993) 811212

16th C. Cotswold stone House

GUEST HOUSE

Tiffany's of Woodstock

36 Oxford Street. Tel: (0993) 811751

RESTAURANTS

The Bear Hotel

Park Street. Tel: (0993) 811511

Brotherton's Brasserie

1 High Street. Tel: (0993) 811114

The Duke of Marlborough

Woodleys. Tel: (0993) 811460

Shabana Restaurant

19 High Street. Tel: (0993) 811017

Vanbrughs

16 Oxford Street. Tel: (0993) 811253

Vickers Hotel & Restaurant

7 Market Place. Tel: (0993) 811212

Wheelers Restaurant

Kings Arms Hotel. Tel: (0993) 811592

PUBLIC HOUSES

The Black Prince

Tel: (0993) 811530

Traditional English 15th century pub with Mexican food.

Free House. Licensee: Mr G Bilbow. Opening Hours: 12 - 2.30 6.30 - 11 Mon-Sat 12-3 7 - 10.30 Sun. Food Available: 12 - 2.30 6.30 - 11 Mon/Sat 12-3 7 - 10.30 Sun. Restaurant Specialities: Mexican/American food. Garden.

The Crown Inn

Tel: (0993) 812570

The Duke of Marlborough

Woodleys. Tel: (0993) 811460

The Kings Head

11 Park Lane. Tel: (0993) 812164

The Punch Bowl

12 Oxford Street. Tel: (0993) 811218

The Queens Own

59 Oxford Street. Tel: (0993) 812414

Licensee: Mr A P Willerton.
The Rose & Crown
81 Manor Road. Tel: (0993) 812009
The Woodstock Arms
8 Market Street. Tel: (0993) 811251

TEA ROOMS
Vanbrughs
16 Oxford Street. Tel: (0993) 811253

OTHER AMENITIES
ART GALLERIES
Craftsmens Gallery
1, Market Street. OX7 1SU Tel: (0993) 811995
Le Print
16, High Street. Tel: (0993) 813021
CARAVAN PARK
Caravan Club Site
Bladon Chains, Bladon Road. Tel: (0993) 812390
HEALTH CLUB
Diet Centre
33, High Street. Tel: (0993) 813341
TOURIST OFFICE
Woodstock Tourist Info Centre
Hensington Road. Tel: (0993) 811038
WINE BAR
Brothertons Wine Bar
1, High Street. Tel: (0993) 811114

🐿 🐿 🐿 🐿 🐿 🐿 🐿

WOOTON
Wooton is an attractive old village situated on the side of a valley above the confluence of the rivers Dorn and Glyme. There are stone-roofed cottages, an Early English church and an elegant Georgian rectory. Akeman Street, the Roman road, passes through the parish. In Wooton there is a road sign warning of toads crossing the road, probably the only one of its kind in the land.
Population: 631. Map Ref: E 6.

CHURCH
St Mary
Built in the 13th century, and added to in the 14th and 15th. There is a stained glass window showing an angel holding the arms of William of Wykeham, founder of New College, Oxford.

HOTEL
The Killingworth Castle
Tel: (0993) 811401

🐿 🐿 🐿 🐿 🐿 🐿 🐿

WORLDS END
Map Ref: E 14.

PUBLIC HOUSE
The Coach & Horses
Tel: (0635) 248743

🐿 🐿 🐿 🐿 🐿 🐿 🐿

WROXTON
Thatched brown ironstone cottages and medieval church surround the duckpond. Wroxton Abbey, on the outskirts, is a grand Elizabethan house built on the site of an Augustinian monastery, owned for many generations by the North family. The house is now owned by an American university. Wroxton is at the centre of the area where iron-mining once flourished, and during the last 100 years it supplied huge quantities of ironstone to South Wales and the Midland steel industries.
Population: 1,993. Map Ref: D 1.

PLACES OF INTEREST
Wroxton Abbey
Tel: (029 573) 551
17th century mansion and gardens, built on the site of 13th century priory. The house possesses three paintings by Holbein, and a quilt sewn by Mary Queen of Scots.

CHURCHES
All Saints
Methodist Chapel
St Thomas of Canterbury (RC)

HOTEL
Wroxton House Hotel
OX15 6QB Tel: (0295) 730482
Picturesque thatched Hotel, candlelit restaurant.

PUBLIC HOUSES
The New Inn
Wroxton Heath. Tel: (029587) 376
The North Arms
Tel: (0295) 730318
Pleasant thatched country inn opposite the abbey, with food to suit all tastes, traditional beers.
Brewery: Wolverhampton & Dudley. Licensee: Mr Thomas E Sylvesta. Opening Hours: 11am - 3.30pm 6.30pm - 11pm. Food Available: 11am - 3.30pm 6.30pm - 11pm. Restaurant Specialities: Home cooked food. Garden.
The White Horse
Tel: (0295) 730223

🐿 🐿 🐿 🐿 🐿 🐿 🐿

THE MILL AT MAPLEDURHAM

WYTHAM

A village comprised of old stone cottages, a lovely inn and a fine Tudor house set in 700 acres, called Wytham Abbey, which is now part of Oxford University. There was never an abbey on this site, but there was once a nunnery in the 7th century.
Population: 152. Map Ref: F 8.

CHURCH
All Saints
The church was completely rebuilt in 1811 and contains some glass from Cumnor Place.

PUBLIC HOUSE
The White Hart Inn
Tel: (0865) 244372
Recommendations: Good Pub Guide.

YARNTON

Situated between Woodstock and Oxford, Yarnton has a large Jacobean manor house and Exeter farm, which used to belong to Exeter college. The manor was built by a branch of the Spencers of Althorp, from whom the Princess of Wales is descended, and their monuments are in the church, where there is a large amount of stained glass .
Population: 2,244. Map Ref: F 7.

CHURCH
St Barthololmew
There are few remains of the original church building dating 1160. The Spencer family restored the church in the 16th century, adding the tower and creating the Spencer Aisle. After still more decline, the church was again restored by William Fletcher, an Oxford draper, in 1793.

INDEX OF ILLUSTRATIONS

CHRIST CHURCH CATHEDRAL, OXFORD

Index of Places of Interest

Broughton Castle (Page 26)

Towns By Map Reference

Town	Map Ref	Pg No
Great Barrington	A 6	50
Burford	A 7	26
Fulbrook	A 7	48
Taynton	A 7	106
Filkins	A 8	47
Kelmscott	A 9	62
Langford	A 9	66
Broadwell	A 9	25
Buscot	A 10	28
Fernham	A 11	46
Ashbury	A 12	11
Little Compton	B 3	67
Little Coxwell	B 3	67
Chastleton	B 4	32
Kingham	B 4	63
Salford	B 4	96
Ascott-Under-Wychwood	B 5	11
Churchill	B 5	35
Milton-under-Wychwood	B 6	74
Shipton-under-Wychwood	B 6	98
Asthall	B 7	12
Swinbrook	B 7	105
Alvescot	B 8	10
Black Bourton	B 8	20
Brize Norton	B 8	25
Carterton	B 8	30
Shilton	B 8	97
Bampton	B 9	14
Clanfield	B 9	35
Radcot	B 9	95
Faringdon	B 10	45
Littleworth	B 10	69
Kingston Lisle	B 11	64
Uffington	B 11	108
Lambourn	B 13	66
Upper Lambourn	B 13	108
Great Rollright	C 3	51
Hook Norton	C 3	60
Little Rollright	C 3	67
Chipping Norton	C 4	33
Chadlington	C 5	30
Charlbury	C 6	31
Finstock	C 6	47
Ramsden	C 6	95
Crawley	C 7	37
Hailey	C 7	54
Minster Lovell	C 7	74
Witney	C 7	114
Curbridge	C 8	38
Ducklington	C 8	42
Lew	C 8	67
Aston	C 9	13
Abingdon	C 10	7
Pusey	C 10	94
Goosey	C 11	49
Sparsholt	C 11	99
Stanford-in-the-Vale	C 11	100
Childrey	C 12	33
Letcombe Bassett	C 12	66
Balscote	D 1	14
Hornton	D 1	60
Shenington	D 1	96
Wroxton	D 1	119
Epwell	D 2	44
Sibford Gower	D 2	98
Swalcliffe	D 2	104
Tadmarton	D 2	105
South Newington	D 3	99
Wigginton	D 3	114
Great Tew	D 4	51
Little Tew	D 4	68
Enstone	D 5	44
Stonesfield	D 6	102
Barnard Gate	D 7	18
Church Hanborough	D 7	35
Freeland	D 7	47
Long Hanborough	D 7	69
New Yatt	D 7	75
North Leigh	D 7	76
South Leigh	D 8	99
Stanton Harcourt	D 8	100
Longworth	D 9	69
Newbridge	D 9	76
Northmoor	D 9	77
Standlake	D 9	99
Charney Bassett	D 10	32
Fyfield	D 10	48
Kingston Bagpuize	D 10	64
Ardington	D 11	11
West Hanney	D 11	112
East Hanney	D 12	11
Letcombe Regis	D 12	67
Wantage	D 12	110
Hanwell	E 1	54
Horley	E 1	60
Broughton	E 2	25
North Newington	E 2	76
Barford St Michael	E 3	18
Bloxham	E 3	23
Milcombe	E 3	73
Middle Barton	E 4	73
Sandford St Martin	E 4	96
The Bartons	E 5	107
Woodstock	E 6	116
Wooton	E 6	119
Bladon	E 7	20
Cassington	E 7	30
Eynsham	E 8	45
North Hinksey	E 8	76
Appleton	E 9	11
Cumnor	E 9	38
Eaton	E 9	43
South Hinksey	E 9	98
Boars Hill	E 9	24
Frilford	E 10	47
Marcham	E 10	72
Frilford Heath	E 10	48
Drayton	E 11	43
East Hendred	E 11	102
Steventon	E 11	102
West Hendred	E 11	112
East Ilsley	E 13	43
West Ilsley	E 13	112
Worlds End	E 14	119
Claydon	F 0	35
Cropredy	F 1	37
Great Bourton	F 1	51
Mollington	F 1	75
Upper Wardington	F 1	108
Wardington	F 1	111
Banbury	F 2	14
Bodicote	F 2	24
Chacombe	F 2	30
Adderbury	F 3	10
Combe	F 3	36
Deddington	F 3	39
Kings Sutton	F 3	64
Milton	F 3	73
Duns Tew	F 4	42
Chesterton	F 5	32
Lower Heyford	F 5	71
Steeple Aston	F 5	101
Tackley	F 5	105
Upper Heyford	F 5	108
Bletchingdon	F 6	20
Enslow	F 6	43
Hampton Poyle	F 6	54
Kirtlington	F 6	66
Shipton-on-Cherwell	F 6	97
Thrupp	F 6	107
Kidlington	F 7	63
Yarnton	F 7	120
Botley	F 8	24
Iffley	F 8	61
Oxford	F 8	78
Wolvercote	F 8	116
Wytham	F 8	120
Rowstock	F 9	96
Sunningwell	F 9	104
Kennington	F 9	62
Chilton	F 10	33
Culham	F 10	38
Radley	F 10	95
Shippon	F 10	97
Appleford	F 11	10
Didcot	F 11	39
Sutton Courtenay	F 11	104
Blewbury	F 12	23
East Hagbourne	F 12	42
Harwell	F 12	54
West Hagbourne	F 12	112
Middleton Cheney	G 2	73
Aynho	G 3	13
Croughton	G 3	37
Fewcott	G 4	47
Fritwell	G 4	48
Souldern	G 4	98
Middleton Stoney	G 5	73
Weston-on-the-Green	G 6	113
Beckley	G 7	18
Islip	G 7	62
Headington	G 8	55
Marston	G 8	72
Summertown	G 8	103
Cowley	G 9	36
Garsington	G 9	48
Littlemore	G 9	68
Sandford-on-Thames	G 9	96
Berinsfield	G 10	18
Clifton Hampden	G 10	36
Nuneham Courtenay	G 10	77
Dorchester-on-Thames	G 11	41
Little Wittenham	G 11	68
Long Wittenham	G 11	69
Aston Tirrold	G 12	13
Aston Upthorpe	G 12	13
North Moreton	G 12	76
South Moreton	G 12	99
Culworth	H 1	38
Cottisford	H 4	36
Hethe	H 4	59
Stoke Lyne	H 4	102
Bicester	H 5	19
Bucknell	H 5	26
Launton	H 5	66
Ambrosden	H 6	10
Arncott	H 6	11
Charlton on Otmoor	H 6	32
Merton	H 6	72
Wendlebury	H 6	112
Ot Moor	H 7	77
Horton-cum-Studley	H 7	61
Forest Hill	H 8	47
Holton	H 8	60
Stanton St John	H 8	101
Waterperry	H 8	111
Wheatley	H 8	113
Cuddesdon	H 9	37
Horspath	H 9	61
Little Milton	H 9	67
Chislehampton	H 10	34
Drayton St Leonard	H 10	42
Stadhampton	H 10	99
Benson	H 11	18
Berrick Salome	H 11	19
Brightwell-cum-Sotwell	H 11	25
Shillingford	H 11	97
Warborough	H 11	111
Crowmarsh Gifford	H 12	37
Ipsden	H 12	61
Wallingford	H 12	109
Goring-on-Thames	H 13	49
Moulsford-on-Thames	H 13	75
Streatley-on-Thames	H 13	103
Goring Heath	H 13	49
Lower Basildon	H 14	70
Pangbourne	H 14	94
Upper Basildon	H 14	108
Whitchurch	H 14	113
Whitchurch Hill	H 14	114
Stratton Audley	I 5	103
Blackthorn	I 6	20
Brill	I 7	25
Great Haseley	I 9	51
Great Milton	I 9	51
Milton Common	I 9	74
Chalgrove	I 10	31
Cuxham	I 10	39
Brightwell Baldwin	I 11	25
Britwell Salome	I 11	25
Ewelme	I 11	44
Nuffield	I 12	77
Hailey	I 12	54
Woodcote	I 13	116
Mapledurham	I 14	71
Fringford	J 4	48
Thame	J 9	106
Lewknor	J 10	67
Pyrton	J 10	95
Christmas Common	J 11	34
Watlington	J 11	111
Maidensgrove	J 12	71
Nettlebed	J 12	75
Russells Water	J 12	96
Fawley	J 12	45
Bix	J 13	20
Peppard Common	J 13	94
Postcombe	J 13	94
Rotherfield Greys	J 13	96
Rotherfield Peppard	J 13	96
Kingwood Common	J 13	66
Highmoor Cross	J 13	60
Binfield Heath	J 14	20
Cuddington	K 7	38
Towersey	K 9	107
Aston Rowant	K 10	13
Chinnor	K 10	33
Kingston Blount	K 10	64
Radnage	K 10	95
Middle Assendon	K 12	73
Stonor	K 12	103
Pishill	K 12	94
Aston (Oxon)	K 12	13
Henley-on-Thames	K 13	56
Lower Assendon	K 13	70
Remenham	K 13	95
Medmenham	K 13	72
Lower Shiplake	K 14	71
Shiplake	K 14	97

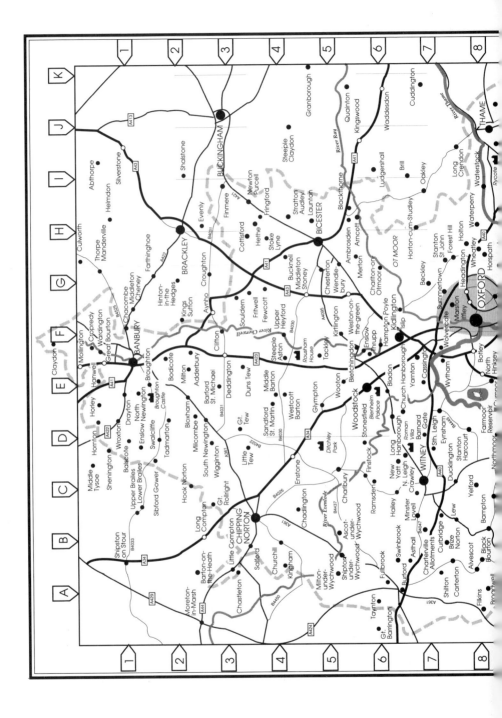

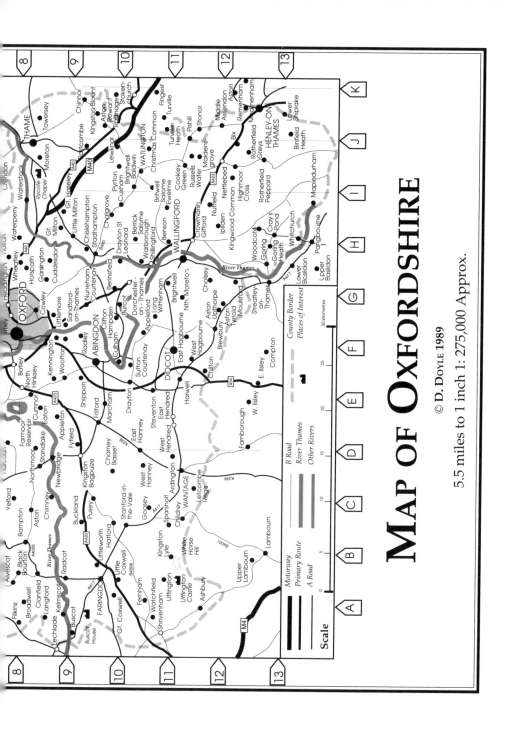

MAP OF OXFORDSHIRE

© D. DOYLE 1989

5.5 miles to 1 inch 1: 275,000 Approx.